a short & happy guide to

Employment Discrimination

Second Edition

Ann C. Juliano
Professor of Law
Villanova University

A SHORT & HAPPY GUIDE® SERIES

WEST ACADEMIC

860 Blue Gentian Road, Suite 350
Eagan, MN 55121
1-877-888-1330

Published in the United States of America

ISBN: 979-8-89545-071-0

For Matt, the Women of Winding Way, and everyone trying to figure out the state of the law

Preface to the Second Edition

You know how you see a remake of a movie and think "did we really need an update to this?" Well, in the area of Employment Discrimination, we definitely needed an update. In the last four years, the Supreme Court issued a number of opinions which changed the relevant tests for issues such as religious accommodation, which transfers count as adverse actions, what must be shown for "reverse" discrimination, and more. Congress passed new statutes and the Equal Employment Opportunity Commission issued guidance for the enforcement. And, as you know unless you have been living under a rock, there has been a change of Presidential Administration. These changes resulted in dueling Executive Orders. Basically, the Biden Administration played an Uno Reverse card on Trump I policies and then the Trump II administration played an Uno Reverse on that Uno Reverse.[1]

So, it is a little tricky to write an update at this point in the world of anti-discrimination law. All recent Supreme Court cases are included as are new statutes. Executive Orders issued by President Trump are noted as well. However, statutes passed by the previous Congress are the subject of litigation and EEOC Guidance has been challenged or revoked. Executive Orders issued by President Biden have been revoked. Executive Orders issued by President Trump have been challenged. I have noted the areas most in flux with "As Of This Writing" or AOTW. If you are using this Short and Happy guide for a class or to write a brief and you are focused on one of these areas, please keep in mind that things may have changed since the publication of this edition.

Enjoy!

---

[1] This is allowed. I looked it up. See UnoRules.com.

Acknowledgments

I'm grateful to Cathy Lanctot who graciously allowed me to take over the Employment Discrimination course back in the day. Thank you to West Academic for allowing me to continue to work on this project. Caroline Harris ('27) provided excellent research assistance on recent developments. Without Congress, the Supreme Court, and changing presidential administrations, there wouldn't be a need for updates. Thanks for all the material.

Table of Contents

A Short & Happy Guide to Employment Discrimination

Second Edition

CHAPTER 1

Introduction to Employment Discrimination

Don't discriminate! That sounds clear enough but as you are learning in your Employment Discrimination course, the implementation of these two words is varied and complex. Understanding the rights of employees and the rights and obligations of employers involves an overlapping system of federal, state, and local laws. If the workplace is a public employer, the U.S. Constitution is involved as well.

What are the challenges facing you as you study Employment Discrimination? In addition to the standard challenges in any subject area, there are a few specific to this area. First, always in the background of the courts' interpretation of the statutes is an attempt at balancing the rights of people to work in an environment free of discrimination with the employer's right to run her workplace the way she chooses. Judges often say that they don't wish to interfere with the employer's judgment unless the action is specifically prohibited by the statute. Second, the courts' interpretation of the statutes changes as their acceptance of the prevalence of discrimination changes. So some of the frameworks created in the 1970s don't appeal as strongly to judges as they once did. It can be confusing to follow the twists and turns of the doctrine so it helps to keep in mind changing societal norms.

In addition, you should recognize that there are employer obligations that give rise to many rights in the workplace that do not fall within the anti-discrimination statutes. For example, workplace safety, the right to worker's compensation, non-compete agreements (and many, many more) are issues that impact an individual worker but are not an issue of discrimination. These topics are covered by the broader area of "Employment Law." This book focuses on one topic within Employment Law—discrimination. Even when we consider the actions in the workplace that may amount to discrimination, those actions may implicate other legal rights as well. For example, sexual harassment violates the federal anti-discrimination statute but may also amount to a tort. Firing an employee because of his religion could be considered a firing against public policy. For purposes of this book (and most likely, your final exam in Employment Discrimination), set those options aside. We are focusing only on the anti-discrimination statutes.

For the most part, courts view the anti-discrimination statutes as *exceptions* to the default rule of letting employers run their workplaces as they see fit. This default rule is known as employment at will. The (almost a cliché) description of employment at will is that an employer may fire an employee for a good reason, a bad reason, or no reason at all (just not a prohibited reason). Conversely, an employee may quit for a good reason, a bad reason, or no reason. So, the default is that the employer can do as she wishes with her workplace.

However, there are various scenarios that can restrict the employer's ability to fire employees. Any time an employer must have "cause" to fire is a restriction on employment at will. An employment contract may contain restrictions. An employer subject to a collective bargaining agreement certainly has restrictions. The civil service system and the tenure system have restrictions on the employer's ability to fire employees on a whim. Finally, some employee handbooks or manuals limit the reasons why an employee may be terminated. This can create a restriction on an employer as well.

Apart from the above scenarios, the employer is able to hire and fire employees "at will," as long as the employer doesn't violate the anti-discrimination statutes. As mentioned above, Employment Discrimination involves many different sources of rights and obligations. Your challenge is to keep track of which statute applies to which factual situation. Fortunately, this book is full of charts and checklists to help you through this maze.

In most courses, you will focus on the "Big Three" anti-discrimination statutes. The Big Three are Title VII of the Civil Rights Act of 1964, the Age Discrimination in Employment Act of 1967, and the Americans with Disabilities Act of 1990 ("ADA"). Title VII prohibits actions taken "because of" race, color, religion, national origin, and sex. The Age Discrimination statute prohibits actions taken "because of" age against someone who is at least 40 years old. Finally, the ADA prohibits actions taken against a qualified individual with a disability. Determining who is entitled to protection under this statute is very complex so the ADA gets its own Chapter.

Under these statutes, the courts have created the frameworks and interpretations that govern in this area and many other areas of the law as well. Some of these other statutes include:

The Equal Pay Act of 1963 (covering compensation and sex discrimination)

The Family and Medical Leave Act of 1993 (covering birth or adoption of a child, serious medical conditions)

The Immigration Reform and Control Act of 1986 (covering national origin, citizenship statute, and documentation to work)

The Genetic Information Non-Discrimination Act of 2008 (covering use of genetic information)

The United Services Employment and Reemployment Rights Act of 1994 (covering membership in or obligation to perform service in a uniformed service)

Section 1981 of the Civil Rights Act of 1866 (covering race in the "mak[ing] and enforce[ement of] contracts")

Section 1983 of the Civil Rights Act of 1871 (covering the violation of a constitutional or statutory right by someone acting under color of state law)

Whew! So now you have a sense of the array of statutes and actions prohibited. As you might imagine, one of the first questions you have to ask yourself is "what statute applies?" There are several other threshold questions as well:

Does this employer fall within the statute? (Do they have enough workers? Are they exempt?)

Does this worker fall within the statute? (Is this person an "employee" or independent contractor?)

Does this employment action fall within the statute? (Did someone get fired or did someone not get the office supplies they wanted?)

Each of these questions is covered in (short and happy) detail in this book. But the biggest question is:

How to prove a violation of the statute?

This is the focus of most Employment Discrimination courses. There are well-established "frameworks" that govern in this area with prima facie cases and defenses unique to each framework. A quick way to distinguish between the frameworks is whether there is intentional discrimination or unintentional discrimination. If the employer intentionally discriminated, the relevant framework is known as "disparate treatment." This might be aimed at one employee (I'm not hiring you because you are a male) or it might be aimed at an entire class of people (I don't think women make good truck drivers so I won't hire them). Unintentional discrimination occurs when the employer has a requirement that is keeping a protected class from the job (you must be 6′ tall to be a firefighter would tend to keep women from the job). Each of these frameworks has its own sets of requirements and relevant defenses. Sometimes, there are multiple options within a single framework! Students often find this aspect of the course the most difficult. Have no fear! Read on.

At this point, you should have a brief idea of the issues ahead. Let's dive in and sort out this interesting, complicated, and emotional topic.

CHAPTER 2

The Basics

Before you begin to wander into the world of burden-shifting and prima facie cases and defenses and lots of acronyms and . . . well, let's step back to make sure the basics are covered. You need a proper defendant, a proper plaintiff, and a covered action.

A. Defendants

The main federal anti-discrimination statutes prohibit action by three types of defendants: employers, labor organizations, and employment agencies.

1. Who Counts as an Employer?

The statutes define an "employer" as a "person engaged in an industry affecting commerce" who has a certain number of employees. If you have already taken Constitutional Law, you know that test is very broad. So, the main limiting factor in this definition is the number of employees. For Title VII and the Americans with Disabilities Act, the employer must have a minimum of 15 employees. For the Age Discrimination in Employment Act, the employer must have a minimum of 20 employees. (In answer to your question, yes, Congress did do this just to make your life more difficult.

To determine if the employer has the minimum number of employees, you need to understand which workers are eligible to be counted. Title VII states that the employer needs 15 or more employees for "each working day for 20 or more calendar weeks in the current or preceding calendar year." If someone is an employee and is on the payroll, they will count toward the minimum number even if they aren't at work that week. Part-time employees who work only a few days a week also count.[1]

Keep in mind that the Supreme Court has held that the minimum number of employees isn't a jurisdictional requirement. In other words, if the employer fails to bring the issue to the court's attention, the court will proceed to decide the claim.

A few random tidbits to keep in mind:

- Under Title VII and the ADEA, the federal government is excluded from the primary definition of "employer" (but don't worry, the Executive Branch is still covered in these statutes).
- For age discrimination (and only age discrimination) claims, state and local governments are covered regardless of the number of employees.
- The federal government as an employer isn't covered by any part of the ADA but is covered by another statute (the Rehabilitation Act).
- Private membership clubs and Indian tribes are also excluded as "employers."

---

[1] There is no minimum number of hours requirement to be considered an employee.

- Certain religious organizations may discriminate on the basis of religion (more on that in Chapter 9).

Finally, there are lots of questions about counting employees—when do separate physical work sites count as a single employer? When do separate workplaces count as joint entity? Going through all the details would make this Short and Happy guide not so short. For now, just know this can be an issue!

2. *Who Counts as a Labor Organization?*

To be covered by the statutes, a labor organization needs to be an "industry affecting commerce." To meet this part of the definition, the labor organization needs to have a hiring hall or a certain minimum number of employees and must meet specific certification requirements. The minimum number of employees is 15 for Title VII and the ADA but 25 for ADEA (I know, I know).

A labor organization must also exist to deal with covered employers (those places discussed above) on issues of employee grievances, labor disputes, wages, rates of pay, hours and other terms and conditions of employment.

3. *Who Counts as an Employment Agency?*

To be a covered employment agency, the person must "procure employees for an employer." In other words, the agency has to refer people who count as "employees" (see below) to workplaces which count as "employers" (see above). The number of employees of the agency is irrelevant. Printing someone else's help wanted ad does not render a newspaper an employment agency. However, your Career Strategy Office does count. This does not mean that the Career Strategy Office is responsible for any discrimination by the employers who use the services of the Office. Rather, the Career Strategy Office cannot itself discriminate.

B. Plaintiffs

Employees, former employees,[2] and job applicants are protected by the statutes. Part-time workers, hourly workers, workers on leave—all these workers may be considered employees. I'm not joking when I tell you the statutory definition of "employee" is "an individual employed by an employer." Honestly. As straightforward (and unhelpful) as this may be, not everyone who works for pay is an "employee." Often, the distinction is between "employee" and "independent contractor."

In Clackamas Gastroenterology Associates, P.C. v. Wells, 538 U.S. 440 (2003), the Supreme Court held that the common law definition of the master-servant relationship governs. The Court listed several factors to consider but the main issue is control by one party over the other. Who supervises the individual? To whom does the individual report? If the organization paying the individual controls their work, then that individual will count as an "employee." If not, then the individual is an independent contractor and excluded from coverage.

The Boss won't count as an employee, unless they function as one. For example, a law firm partner (or executive or Board member) is typically considered the "employer" unless they are treated the same as an associate. In that case, they might be considered an "employee."

Usually you need to be actually PAID to count as an employee. Therefore, typically, volunteers, students, and interns don't count as employees.[3] But (there's always a "but") if the person receives a

---

[2] There is a caveat to the former employees category. Because the decision is based in the language of the Americans with Disabilities Act, this is discussed in Chapter 11.

[3] You should be aware that some states are enacting specific laws to protect interns and volunteers from workplace harassment. Always check the state and local statutes!

certain level of indirect benefits, they might be considered an employee.

When in Rome . . . it depends on whether you are Roman or working for a US company. US citizens working abroad for US companies are covered by federal statutes (unless working where that violates local law). Non-US citizens working abroad for US companies are NOT covered. Non-citizens working in the US for a US company are covered.

C. What Employment Actions Count? (i.e. Do I Have a Case if You Took My Red Stapler?)

Hiring, firing, refusing to hire, paying someone less—these actions are unquestionably covered. After all, the statutory language prohibits employers from "failing or refusing to hire or to fire any individual." The statutes also prohibit discrimination in compensation. So paying an employee less because of a prohibited reason is covered.

The statutes, however, go beyond these actions, to prohibit "discriminat[ion] with respect to . . . terms, conditions, or privileges of employment." Courts have interpreted this language to require an "adverse employment action" and further the action needs to be materially adverse. "Adverse" doesn't mean the employer is cackling and acting with evil intent. Losing a promotion, getting demoted, being transferred with a loss in pay—these are all adverse actions.

Transfers usually present the trickiest situations. Sometimes a transfer comes with a loss of pay or rank. Those cases are more straightforward and fall within an adverse action. However, with some transfers, there is not an obvious demotion or reduction in pay. Imagine an employee moved from one location to another. When should those transfers be considered an adverse action? The

Supreme Court addressed this question in Muldrow v. City of St. Louis, 601 U.S. 346 (2024), and adopted a standard that does not require a showing of "significant harm." Rather, the Court held that a plaintiff under Title VII must show "some harm respecting an identifiable term or condition of employment" but that the harm does not need to be "significant." So a police officer who was removed from her plainclothes position, was assigned to more weekend shifts, and lost access to a department car may be able to show the necessary level of harm.

So, in answer to the above question, you probably cannot sue if your employer takes your red stapler.

Further, there does not need to be an economic harm. Because the statutes use the language "terms, conditions, and privileges" of employment, employers are forbidden from making your workplace a nasty place to work because of the protected classes. This is known as a hostile work environment. (See Chapter 9).

In addition to all of the actions discussed above, there are restrictions specific to unions. Unions cannot refuse membership to or expel someone from the union because of membership in the protected class. A union also is prohibited from causing the employer to engage in unlawful conduct (i.e. refuse to hire people because of their race). Employment agencies cannot refuse to refer people to employers because of protected characteristics. And those signs from days of old—No Irish Need Apply—are prohibited. All three types of defendants are forbidden from publishing ads or notices that limit employment on a prohibited basis.

There is another type of employment action known as accommodation. This involves changing the job in some way and employers have to accommodate religious practices, known disabilities, and—sometimes—pregnant workers. But there is (of course!) a whole new set of tests and whatnot for accommodations. We'll discuss that in later Chapters.

To summarize:

Once you have decided if the workplace counts as an EMPLOYER, the individual counts as an EMPLOYEE, and the action at issue counts as a COVERED ACTION (*Widgets, Inc, with 100 employees fires Pat, a full-time employee*), then you have to decide if and how Pat can prove that they were fired BECAUSE OF membership in a protected class.

Moving on . . .

CHAPTER 3

Individual Disparate Treatment

A brief note on the concept of frameworks:

Just as there are a myriad of ways to violate the anti-discrimination statutes, there are several frameworks to prove those violations. Which framework to apply depends on the evidence available and the underlying violation. These frameworks come in to play most often prior to trial, as a way to test the evidence on a summary judgment motion. The Supreme Court has made clear that the frameworks are not pleading standards (ooohhhh, Civil Procedure).[1]

The first, and most common, framework is the Individual Disparate Treatment framework. This is the appropriate framework when an employee believes he has been treated adversely because of his membership in a protected class. For any claim that is a treatment claim, the plaintiff must prove intent (intent to treat differently, not evil cackling intent). In other words, the employee

1 Swierkiewicz v. Sorema N.A., 534 U.S. 506 (2002).

must show that the employer didn't hire her because she's female or you fired me because I'm Black.

Within the individual disparate treatment claim, there are two different frameworks: 1) single motive or pretext; and, 2) mixed motive. The phrase "single motive" refers to a case the litigation comes down to a but for situation: the plaintiff must prove that but for the plaintiff's race, she would not have been fired.[2] The employer will, of course, offer a reason for the employment action (failure to properly fill out paperwork). Mixed motive refers to a situation wherein there is evidence that the employer had multiple reasons, one of which is the plaintiff's membership in the protected class (you were late to work and you're Catholic). Let's begin with the single motive framework.

A. Single Motive

As with most civil litigation, a plaintiff has the burden of proving that the employer has violated the statute. Early in the days of Title VII, the Court recognized that it is not often (but more common than one would think!) that there is a statement from the employer "I see that you are Asian [or any other protected class], and I shall not hire you because of that." When there is such a statement, the plaintiff has all the evidence she needs to establish a violation of the statute.[3] The defendant is left to offer an alternative explanation or assert a statutory defense.

But most of the time, there isn't a memo or statement. In recognition of this, the Court created a framework to prove a case through circumstantial evidence. The Court set forth a three part

---

[2] The Court in Comcast Corp. v. National Association of African-Owned Media, 589 U.S. 327 (2020), held that section 1981 claims require a showing of "but for" causation.

[3] Of course, this is assuming lots of things—the person actually made the statement, the person who made the statement is a decision maker, the statement was made in the context of the decision making, so on and so forth.

burden shifting framework in McDonnell Douglas Corp. v. Green, 411 U.S. 792 (1973). The framework is known as . . . wait for it . . . the *McDonnell Douglas* framework.[4]

1. Where It All Begins—the Prima Facie Case

The first part of the framework starts with the plaintiff's prima facie case (PFC). One goal of the PFC is to rule out the most common reasons for turning down an applicant. If I applied to be a neurosurgeon, I would *not* get that job (one would hope)—because I am not qualified. If someone applied to teach Civil Procedure and Employment Discrimination at Villanova, they would *not* get the job (one would hope)—because there isn't an open position.

Traditionally, the five elements of the PFC are:

1. Membership in the protected class.

   In *McDonnell Douglas,* the Court labeled this element as "member of a racial minority" but in a later case (Texas Dep't of Community Affairs v. Burdine, 450 U.S. 248 (1981)), the Court made clear the elements are flexible and may vary depending on the facts of the case. So, for this first element, a plaintiff would simply allege: male, female,[5] religion, race,[6] national origin; over 40;[7] qualified individual with a disability.

   A plaintiff does not have to be a member of a historically disadvantaged group. In other words, a sex discrimination claim could be brought by a man or a race

---

[4] When considering whether this framework applies to 42 U.S.C. § 1981, the Supreme Court was weirdly reluctant to hold that it does. Comcast Corp. v. National Association of African-Owned Media, 589 U.S. 327 (2020).

[5] *See* Chapter 9 for a discussion of what is covered by the term "sex."

[6] 42 U.S.C. § 1981 prohibits race discrimination in the making and enforcement of contracts.

[7] The plaintiff needs to be someone over 40 discriminated against in favor of someone younger (General Dynamics v. Cline, 540 U.S. 581 (2004)).

discrimination claim could be brought by a white employee. In addition, a plaintiff is still able to establish a prima facie case even if the discriminatory action was taken by someone in the same protected class (for example, a woman is fired by a woman).

2. Qualified for the position in question.

At this stage, the plaintiff doesn't need to prove that he is the MOST qualified applicant for the job. He just needs to show that he meets the minimal qualifications, that is whatever qualifications the employer announced. If the plaintiff has been fired, then she simply states that she was performing her job at adequate levels. Now, if you think the qualifications announced by the employer are discriminatory (you must be 5′10″ to have a job here), well, this isn't the framework for you. Go read Chapter 5.

3. Applied for an open position.

Yes, I know, it's shocking. But to prove a claim that someone refused to hire you because of your religion, you must prove that you actually applied. As long as the plaintiff makes some showing to the employer of interest in the job, this is usually enough to meet this element of the PFC. Further, you have to apply for an *open* position. Maybe the employer placed an ad with a job search site. Or even told their employees to ask their friends if they would like to apply. If the case is a termination case, then this element doesn't apply.

4. Adverse employment action.

Despite the fact that the statutes use the word "discrimination," courts have interpreted this language to require the plaintiff to have suffered an adverse employment action. "Ultimate employment actions" will certainly suffice—not being hired, getting fired, denied a promotion. A transfer might be an adverse employment action, depending on the details (Loss of pay? Benefits? Opportunity for trainings?). Working longer hours for the same pay will be considered an adverse employment action. But handing out different color pens based on sex will not be an adverse employment action.

5. The job was filled with someone outside of the protected class.

 Obviously, this isn't the only way to meet this element because what if the position remained open and the employer kept searching? Or what if the employer eliminated the position? Some courts have phrased this element as "circumstances giving rise to an inference of discrimination."

Because the elements vary so greatly with each factual scenarios (hiring v. firing; the position is filled v. the position isn't filled), some courts have simplified these elements to three:

1) plaintiff is a member of a protected class under the statute;

2) there was an adverse employment action;

3) in circumstances giving rise to an inference of discrimination.

Regardless of the phrasing, here's the important part: once the plaintiff establishes the prima facie case, a presumption of discrimination is created. The theory is this: a qualified individual applies for an open position and the employer fills it with someone outside of that protected class.

PFC PROVEN = PRESUMPTION OF DISCRIMINATION

But it is only a presumption. Once the PFC is established, the burden shifts to the employer.

2. *The Legitimate Non-Discriminatory Reason*

Because of the presumption created by the PFC, if the employer remains silent, the plaintiff wins. Guess how many times the employer has remained silent? Exactly—never.

The employer must "articulate" a legitimate non-discriminatory reason for the employment action. There are two parts to consider: what does articulate mean and what counts as a legitimate non-discriminatory reason. According to the Court, "articulate" means that the employer simply has a burden of production. In other words, the burden is not a burden of proof. The employer doesn't have to convince the judge or the jury that the reason it offers is actually the reason for the employment action. There just needs to be some admissible evidence produced on the reason (the Human Resources Director could make a statement). The idea here to raise an issue that the plaintiff was not hired for some reason apart from his race/age/etc. (based on the claim).

Now what counts as a legitimate non-discriminatory reason? Consider the following list of reasons in response to a claim for discrimination because of religion.

- "you don't like dogs"
- "you're an Aquarius"
- "you're not qualified"
- "you're not a good fit, personality-wise"
- "you lack leadership skills"
- "you're too old"

Which of these reasons would meet the burden of the defendant in the claim for religious discrimination? . . . . ALL OF THEM.

The reason articulated by the defendant doesn't have to be related to the job. The employer can fire someone because they don't like dogs—even if the employer isn't a vet. The reasons could be subjective (personality) or nonsensical (Aquarius). In fact, the reason could be unlawful ("you're too old"), as long as it isn't a reason based on the protected class at issue.[8] In addition, an employer might be mistaken. For example, maybe the employer thought the applicant doesn't have a college degree but the applicant does in fact have a college degree. If the employer makes an "honest mistake," and the fact finder believes the employer, then there is no discriminatory intent.

Yes, I know what you're thinking: "legitimate" does not really make sense. You are correct. Some courts use the term "non-discriminatory reason" but many still use the term "legitimate non-discriminatory reason" a.k.a. "LNDR."

If the employer meets this extremely onerous burden (that's some sarcasm right there), the presumption of discrimination will be dropped from the case. The burden now shifts back to the plaintiff to prove what's known as pretext.

3. *Where the Rubber Hits the Road: Pretext*

Stop for a moment and consider where we are in this framework: suppose the plaintiff has shown that he is qualified and he didn't get the job in circumstances that might indicate religious discrimination. The employer has offered up a different reason that he didn't get the job—perhaps his personality wasn't suited to the position. At this final stage, the plaintiff needs to prove that the employer acted because of his religion, not because of his personality. In other words, the "it's your personality" explanation

---

[8] Although such a statement would indicate a violation of the ADEA, a plaintiff may not be able to recover due to the procedural requirements for claims. See Chapter 12.

is not the real reason for the refusing to hire him. The real reason, the *determinative* factor, is the plaintiff's membership in the protected class. So, in this hypothetical, religion is the determinative factor in the decision.

It's important to know that the plaintiff doesn't win just because he proves the employer lied about the LNDR. The Court has held that proving the LNDR isn't the real reason is NOT the same as the employer never producing an LNDR. The plaintiff still has the burden to prove that the employer acted "because of" a prohibited reason. It's possible that the employer lied about this because the employer was trying to cover up some other (non-discriminatory) reason. Maybe the employer is trying to keep the job open for his niece, for example. In other words, proof by the plaintiff that the LNDR isn't the real reason doesn't mean the plaintiff automatically wins. St. Mary's Honor Center v. Hicks, 509 U.S. 502 (1993).

After the Court decided the *Hicks* case, some lower courts decided this meant the plaintiff always had to have evidence beyond proving the LNDR was false. In other words, plaintiffs had to show "pretext plus:" prove the LNDR is a pretext *plus* more evidence to prove that membership in the protected class is the determinative factor in the employment action. If the plaintiff's evidence merely established the prima facie case and showed the LNDR was false, the "pretext plus" standard meant the plaintiff would automatically lose.

In Reeves v. Sanderson Plumbing, 530 U.S. 133 (2000), the Court said not so fast, lower courts, we didn't mean the plaintiff *always* loses with that evidence. The Court reiterated that the plaintiff must show the ultimate burden that his protected class is the determinative factor in the employment action. But, the Court made clear, it is possible that the plaintiff's evidence to make out a prima facie case together with the evidence that the reason offered by the employer is false is strong enough to prove this ultimate burden.

PFC evidence

+ proving the LNDR false

= enough to show discriminatory intent (maybe)

To repeat: PFC evidence plus evidence that the LNDR is false *MAY* be sufficient to prove that the plaintiff's protected class is the determinative factor in the employment action.

What remains true is that the plaintiff must show that the employer had the requisite intent to treat him differently (and adversely) because of his protected class. What types of evidence may help make this showing? The possibilities are broad:

- The employer's prior treatment of the plaintiff
- Negative comments about the protected class
- The employer's treatment of other members in the protected class
- The demographics of the workplace
- The employer's failure to follow procedures
- Changing reasons offered for the decision
- Difference in qualifications between the successful applicant and the plaintiff

This last category of evidence, a difference in qualifications, is some of the most probative evidence a plaintiff may offer. It is sometimes known as "comparator" evidence. Although a plaintiff isn't required to show that he was the most qualified applicant, if he can show that he has superior qualifications to the person selected, this is certainly probative evidence. However, lower courts required a big difference between qualifications to establish pretext, a difference they used to describe as one that "jumps off the page and slaps you in face." Seriously, that was the phrase. The Supreme Court in Ash v. Tyson's Foods, 546 U.S. 454 (2006), told the lower courts that wasn't helpful and to come up with something better (which, in itself, is not helpful). Now the courts look to see if a reasonable and impartial decision maker would have selected the successful applicant over the plaintiff.

4. "Reverse" Discrimination

Courts are clear that the *McDonnell Douglas* framework applies in single motive cases under Title VII. However, many lower courts had altered the elements somewhat in cases involving claims of "reverse" discrimination. In these cases, the plaintiff is a member of the "majority" group (i.e. White, male, straight) and brings a claim alleging that they have been discriminated against on the basis of membership in that group. In order to find the presumption of discrimination, these courts required plaintiffs to allege "background circumstances" to prove that their employer is the unusual employer who discriminates against the majority. For example, either the decision-making was a member of a minority group or there was a pattern of discrimination against majority group members.

The Supreme Court, in 9-0 (!!) decision ruled that requiring this heightened showing is not supported by the text of Title VII nor Supreme Court precedents. In Ames v. Ohio Department of Youth Services, 605 U.S. 303 (2025), the plaintiff alleged she was denied a promotion and then demoted because she is straight when the position she sought went to a lesbian and her previous job went to a gay man. The Court made clear that the test is the same regardless of the plaintiff's membership in a majority or minority group.

5. *A Brief Note on Cats and Monkeys (Yes, Cats and Monkeys)*

Sometimes, one person in the workplace has the discriminatory intent but another person takes the adverse employment action. For example, suppose your immediate supervisor keeps reporting you as late to work because she doesn't like your national origin. Then the Human Resources Director reviews the documentation and terminates you for excessive tardiness. One employee has the intent and used her position to get another employee to take an adverse action. Is a plaintiff out of luck? Not necessarily. In this fact pattern, described by the Court as a "cat's paw" scenario,[9] the employer is liable if a supervisor acts with discriminatory animus (dislike of your national origin) and she intends that act to cause an adverse employment action (hopefully this will get you fired), and that act is a proximate cause of the ultimate employment action (HR Director terminates you based on the tardiness reports alone).[10]

To summarize the basic structure for a single motive case:

Plaintiff proves PFC.

Defendant articulates LNDR.

Plaintiff proves Pretext: the LNDR is a lie and the real reason (the determinative factor) is his membership in a protected class.

PFC ⟶ LNDR ⟶ Pretext

Are you exhausted yet? But wait, there's more . . .

---

[9] According to this Aesop's Fable, a monkey flatters his friend the cat as a means to encourage the cat to reach into a fire to bring out some delicious roasting chestnuts. The monkey eats the chestnuts and the cat ends up with burned paws. Presumably, the supervisor who takes the adverse action is the cat.

[10] Staub v. Proctor Hospital, 562 U.S. 411 (2011). This isn't a case under one of the Big Three employment discrimination statutes but the standard has been adopted by lower courts in Title VII cases. (Plus, this case is discussed in most employment discrimination casebooks!).

B. Mixed Motive

The second way to prove an individual disparate treatment case is through what is known as the "mixed motive" structure. This type of fact pattern applies when the employment action is taken for both legitimate *and* discriminatory reasons. For example, suppose the employer tells an applicant, "you have a bad personality; plus, you are Italian-American. So, you know, we aren't going to hire you." Bad personality is a non-discriminatory reason but the decision is also based on national origin. This is a mixed motive case.

The Supreme Court first recognized this type of claim in Price Waterhouse Coopers v. Hopkins, 490 U.S. 228 (1989). There, the plaintiff had direct evidence that she was denied partnership because of her sex.[11] A plurality of the Court held that Ann Hopkins' direct evidence of sex was enough to prove that sex played a motivating factor in the decision and that was enough to establish liability. However, the trial court also found that the employer relied on comments by partners that Hopkins was abrasive and had trouble managing staff. Responding to this multiple motive scenario, the Court held that Price Waterhouse could avoid liability only if it could prove that it would have taken the same action without considering the plaintiff's sex.

To rephrase, once the plaintiff shows that the employer was motivated, even in part, by a prohibited factor, the employer avoids liability entirely if it proves that it would have made the "same decision" absent consideration of the prohibited factor. Justice O'Connor concurred with the outcome and the concept of a mixed motive framework but she required that the prohibited factor be a "substantial factor" in the decision.

---

[11] Seriously. You should read the case. "Macho," "should take a course at charm school," "needs to wear more make-up and jewelry," I could go on.

Two years after the *Price Waterhouse* decision, Congress amended Title VII and, among other things, added language to make clear that there is a violation of Title VII if a plaintiff "demonstrates that race, color, religion, sex, or national origin was a motivating factor" for the employment action, even if other factors also motivated the action.[12]

Congress didn't completely do away with the idea of the "same decision" defense from *Price Waterhouse*. Under the amendment, if an employer proves that it would have made the same decision in the absence of the impermissible reason, then the available remedies are limited (but there is still liability).[13] This is section 706(g).

Under this amended version of Title VII, once a plaintiff proves the protected class was a motivating factor in the employment action, the employer has violated the statute. The only question is whether the employer will be able to limit the remedies with the same decision defense. To repeat, even if the employer proves the same decision defense, it is *still* liable. To be clear, THIS IS DIFFERENT FROM *PRICE WATERHOUSE*.

C. Across the Statutes

Now, I know what you're thinking: "why did you make me learn about the *Price Waterhouse* decision if I could just cite to the statute?" Well, the *Price Waterhouse* framework isn't completely irrelevant. In fact, each of the three main anti-discrimination statutes has its own framework.

---

[12] This is known as the § 703(m) instruction.

[13] If a defendant carries this burden, then the court may grant "declaratory relief, injunctive relief, attorney's fees and costs but shall not award damages, reinstatement, hiring or promotion." Section 706(g).

Title VII: The motivating factor and same decision defense structure explained above applies to Title VII, except for retaliation claims.[14]

The Age Discrimination in Employment Act: The Supreme Court in Gross v. FBL Financial Services, Inc., 557 U.S. 167 (2009), held that the mixed motive framework isn't available under the ADEA. Basically, the Court focused on the absence of the motivating factor language in the ADEA.

The Americans with Disabilities Act: Frankly, this is a bit of a mess. The Supreme Court hasn't squarely decided the causation standards under the ADA and the lower courts are split. There are three possibilities. First, cases must meet the "but for" causation standard as set forth in *Gross*. The trend in the circuit courts is in this direction. The rest of the Circuits are split between applying the Title VII framework (liability established at the point where the plaintiff shows the protected class was a motivating factor) and applying the *Price Waterhouse* framework (liability avoided if the employer can prove it would have made the "same decision.").

To view it another way:

	Title VII 703(a) claims	Retaliation claims	ADEA	ADA
703(m) framework	★	✗	✗	?

[14] See Chapter 7.

	Title VII 703(a) claims	Retaliation claims	ADEA	ADA
Price Waterhouse framework	✗	✗	✗	?
NOPE—no mixed motive claim available	✗	★	★	?

Now that you have the two frameworks in mind (single motive/ pretext and mixed motive), you should be thinking "when do I use which one?" Many lower courts decided (based on Justice O'Connor's concurrence in *Price Waterhouse*) that direct evidence was the decision point for choosing between the mixed or single motive frameworks. Direct evidence, broadly, means evidence that proves the point without having to draw any inferences to get there. (In a memo, the employer states "don't hire him because he's Black.") In other words, if the plaintiff had direct evidence that she was fired because of her religion, then she could proceed under the mixed motive framework.

After a few years of this, the Supreme Court held in Desert Palace, Inc. v. Costa, 539 U.S. 90 (2003), that direct evidence isn't required to make use of the mixed motive framework. Instead, the Court held that a plaintiff needs sufficient evidence, direct or circumstantial, to show that the protected class was a motivating factor in the decision. *Desert Palace* created quite a bit of confusion. In general, whether the jury receives a "motivating factor" instruction or a "but for/determinative factor" instruction depends on the evidence presented. Although a plaintiff may choose to plead and litigate his case under only one framework, courts have allowed plaintiffs to present under both all the way up to and including trial. The trial judge then determines the appropriate framework at the close of all the evidence.

That is quite a bit of information—and we are only on the first type of claim! I promise that it gets easier from here on out. The individual treatment claim is the most complicated of the framework schemes.

CHAPTER 4

Systemic Disparate Treatment

An individual disparate treatment claim focuses on how one individual has been treated. The systemic disparate treatment claim addresses an employer who discriminates on a class-wide basis. As a treatment claim,[1] the plaintiffs must show intent on the part of the employer. There are two methods to prove this claim: a facially discriminatory policy and a pattern or practice of discrimination.

A. Facial Policy of Discrimination

This is straightforward: the employer has a policy which discriminates on its face.

- You must be a woman to be waitstaff at the TinyShirtsAndHotPants restaurant.
- You must be Irish to be a bartender at the Irish Pub.

1 Recall from Chapter 1 that there are treatment claims which require a showing of intent and there are impact claims that do not require a showing of intent. We'll discuss impact claims in the next Chapter.

- You must be Catholic to teach at the parochial school.
- You must be younger than 50 to work as sales associate.

The only thing the plaintiff needs to prove is that the policy 1) mandates or allows 2) actions covered by the statute 3) on the basis of a protected class covered by the statute. That's it, that's the entire prima facie case. In other words, taking an example from the list above, you must [mandated] be a woman [protected class under Title VII] to be hired as waitstaff [actions covered by the statute]. At this point, the employer avoids liability only with a statutory defense (discussed below).

B. Pattern or Practice of Discrimination

1. *The Prima Facie Case*

When there isn't a facially discriminatory policy but few people in the protected class are hired (or promoted), there might be a pattern or practice claim.[2] As courts have explained it, under this type of claim, a plaintiff shows it is the employer's standard operating procedure to discriminate against the protected class. In other words, the plaintiffs must prove that the employer has the intent to discriminate against the protected class. Let's consider Widgets, Inc. and Black employees. When there isn't a facial policy, how can plaintiffs prove the employer's intent against an entire class? Numbers. Lots and lots of numbers. In fact, in these cases, the employer's intent to discriminate is inferred from the numbers. What??, you say, I was promised no math in law school! Yes, well, my apologies.

---

[2] These cases are primarily litigated as class actions or brought by the EEOC.

The basic idea behind the numbers is this: there is a big disparity between who has the job at issue (the current employees) and who lives and works in the surrounding area (potential employees). The presumption is that an employer who is NOT discriminating will have a workforce that is more or less representative of the population in the surrounding community. When the disparity is big enough, that may be enough to prove a prima facie case of intent to discriminate. For example, 1% of the employees at Widgets, Inc. are Black but the surrounding geographic area is 80% Black. The Supreme Court held in International Brotherhood of Teamsters v. U.S., 431 U.S. 324 (1977), that when the disparity is this large, the statistics alone may prove the prima facie case. Further, even when the numbers aren't quite so stark,[3] a statistical analysis may still meet the burden.

Buckle up and bear with me for a minute as we take a quick detour back to your undergrad Stats class. There's a measurement known as a standard deviation. A standard deviation is a way to quantify how unlikely a result is to occur as a matter of chance. Think of a bell curve. How likely is it that the number of Black employees at Widgets (1%) happened as a matter of chance, without some other force being involved? And by "some other force," we mean discrimination. The Court held in Hazelwood School District v. U.S., 433 U.S. 299 (1977), that any result outside of 2 or 3 standard deviations is enough to meet the prima face case. A result this far off the expected results (keep that Bell curve in your mind) seems fishy. And by fishy, we mean, is a result of discrimination.

The key to the prima facie case is choosing the comparison group. The number of people in the protected class in the job is always one group. The real question is how to select the other group. There are a few options. Using the applicant pool as the comparison group is always probative. If 40% of the applicant pool

[3] Stark as in drastic, not as in Arya.

is Black but only 1% of the Widgets' employees, that would be a strong prima facie case! But sometimes, the applicant pool is skewed. If word on the street is that Widgets discriminates, perhaps Black potential employees won't even bother applying. In such cases, the comparison group could be workers in the surrounding area. Many factors can go into determining this appropriateness of this group but an easy rule of thumb is to consider the geographic location of the current employees prior to hiring. In addition, if the job at issue requires a certain degree or license (a teacher, a commercial truck driver), then the comparison group must be limited to those people with that degree or license.

Nothing brings life to boring numbers like some human interest stories. In addition to statistics, plaintiffs gather testimony from people in the protected class of their failed attempts to be hired at Widgets. Finally, the history of Widgets' treatment and hiring of Black employees is also helpful to establish the prima facie case.

That's the prima face case for a pattern or practice claim:

1) protected class under the statute

2) adverse action

3) employer's standard operating procedure is to discriminate

2. *Defendant's Rebuttal*

Although not technically a "defense" in the burden-shifting manner of a defense, an employer may allows challenge the basis of the plaintiff's case. For example, the employer could argue that the plaintiffs should have used the applicant pool as the comparison group or they didn't narrow the comparison group by the people possessing the required license. In addition, employers sometimes acknowledge the disparity but then provide some reason other than discrimination to explain it. "Yup, that is one big disparity right there. But we aren't discriminating against women. We have a veterans' hiring preference and more veterans are men." If you read Personnel Administrator v. Feeney, 442 U.S. 256 (1979), in Con Law, that should sound familiar to you.[4] Or "no, no, it's not us, it's them! Sure, there's a huge disparity but it's because women don't want these jobs." This is known as the lack of interest defense. If the plaintiff is able to prove the prima facie case, most likely the employer is going to assert a statutory defense.

3. BFOwhat?

Title VII and the ADEA[5] allow an employer to facially discriminate in hiring (yes, I do mean flat out discriminate) when it can establish that age (ADEA, § 4(f)) or sex, religion, or national origin (Title VII, § 703(e)) is a "bona fide occupational qualification reasonably necessary to the normal operation of the particular business." Whew, that's a mouthful! That's probably why most people just call it a BFOQ. Because this defense allows facial discrimination, it is narrowly interpreted and rarely found.

Look over that list again. Notice anything . . . RACE and COLOR are not on the list. The statute does not allow for a race based BFOQ.[6]

Any time the employer has a facially discriminatory policy ("you must be female to have this job" or "you must not be Italian"), the only defense available is a BFOQ. Because a BFOQ allows the employer to discriminate, the defense is limited to situations where the job qualification relates to the essence or to the central mission of the employer's business. So, unlike the

---

4 FYI—Title VII exempts veterans' preference policies from the statute.

5 The ADEA doesn't have an explicit BFOQ defense but it does allow other standards and qualifications. See Chapter 11.

6 Despite this, courts have allowed hiring on race based terms for a small, limited number of cases. For instance, casting for a show or for safety reasons for law enforcement.

legitimate non-discriminatory reason from the individual claim, this defense must be necessary to the business. For example, requiring an exotic dancer at a club with female exotic dancers to be female would go to the "central mission" of the employer's business.

Sometimes, the employer is using the BFOQ as a proxy for something else, often safety. In one case the Court considered, a prison required guards in certain areas to be male. The Court upheld the BFOQ because it found that women would cause a risk to other guards and inmates. Sometimes, the BFOQ is based on age and the employer's underlying concern is health (please don't have a heart attack while you are flying the airplane). In these cases, the employer must meet a test the Court set forth in *Criswell v. Western Airlines:*

> 1) there is reasonable cause to believe that all or substantially all of the persons in the class are unable to perform safely and efficiently duties of the job; or
>
> 2) some employees in the class possess a trait precluding safe and efficient job performance, and it is practically impossible for the employer to deal with the class of employees on an individual basis.

Generally, courts hold that BFOQs cannot be defended on grounds of customer preference, increased costs, or as a marketing plan but may sometimes be based on privacy concerns (attendant in a bathroom, nurses for elderly patients in nursing home), authenticity (bartender at the Irish pub), and, as mentioned, safety (9 month pregnant flight attendant). I like to think of two examples from my own life: room moms and backstage moms. When my kids were in elementary school, there were "room moms" who planned the class parties. If the room moms fell within Title VII (which they don't but just play along), truly there is no need for the person who assigns who is bringing popcorn to the party to be female. However, backstage moms at the dance recital do need to be female because there are girls changing costumes in various states of undress.[7]

C. Avoidance of Disparate Impact Liability as a Defense

The one confusing defense in a systemic disparate treatment case involves the disparate impact claim discussed in the next Chapter. Without making you go read the next Chapter and come back, here's the relevant description of an impact claim: the employer has a neutral requirement (like a test) and a protected class in adversely impacted by that requirement (only 20% of Latinx applicants pass the test but 80% of White applicants pass). Keep that in mind as we consider how they might interact.

The New Haven Fire Department gave a written test for promotions. The results were such that few Black or Hispanic fire fighters would have been promoted. The City tossed out the results of the test. The people who would have been promoted under the results of the test sued and alleged systemic disparate treatment. The City argued that they had a defense because they were trying to avoid liability under an impact claim.

In Ricci v. DeStefano, 557 U.S. 557 (2009), the Court held that an employer may engage in disparate treatment to avoid disparate impact liability "only when the employer has a strong basis in evidence to believe that it will be subject to disparate impact liability if it fails to take the race-conscious action." The key word here is liability. It's not enough that the employer thinks it might get sued. It has to have a good basis in evidence that it will lose.

[7] Yes, there were backstage dads for the boys in the recital.

D. Voluntary Affirmative Action

One last issue specific to disparate treatment claims is voluntary affirmative action plans.[8] Because affirmative action plans consider race or sex or national origin in employment decisions, they are subject to challenge under Title VII. Plus, if the employer is a public employer, there are possible claims under both Title VII and the Equal Protection Clause.

1. The Constitution

This isn't the Short and Happy Guide to the Constitution so this will be VERY short. As the Equal Protection doctrine currently stands, race classifications by a state actor are reviewed under the strict scrutiny standard and sex based classifications are reviewed under a heightened scrutiny standard, regardless of motivation. In applying the "compelling" or "important" governmental interest prong, the Court has found the need to remedy past segregation by that governmental actor as a compelling state interest. However, the Court, in considering the use of race, severely restricted the use of affirmative action in education. Students for Fair Admissions v. President and Fellows of Harvard College, 600 U.S. 181 (2023).

2. Title VII

The Court has a different test under Title VII for affirmative action. In United Steelworkers of America v. Weber, 443 U.S. 193 (1979), the Court upheld the ability of employers to adopt voluntary, race- or sex-conscious affirmative action plans. Against the argument that this type of decision violates Title VII, the Court held affirmative action plans meet the spirit and purpose of the statute. The Court attempted to balance possible liability to Black

---

[8] "Voluntary" means that the employer adopted the plan in the absence of a court order.

plaintiffs who were underrepresented at the workplace with possible liability to White employees for "reverse discrimination." To find the balance, the Court created a three part test (shocking! A three part test!). First and foremost, there needs to be an actual plan (not some idea from Wanda in HR). Then the plan:

1. must aim to remedy a manifest imbalance
2. in traditionally segregated job categories
3. and cannot unduly trammel the rights of disfavored groups.

Without going into all the details on each part of the test, there needs to be a large (obvious) imbalance to support an affirmative action but it doesn't have to reach the level of proving a prima facie case of a systemic disparate treatment. Also, it doesn't matter if the imbalance is created by the employer itself (as required under the Equal Protection Clause) or rather by societal norms and expectations. Finally, to meet the last prong, the plan shouldn't create an absolute right to the job in question, shouldn't be in place forever, and should have short term and long term goals.

The counter intuitive part of affirmative action plans involves the litigation process. In an individual disparate treatment case, a plaintiff will prove the elements needed for a prima facie case (you didn't hire me because of my race). In a systemic disparate treatment case, the plaintiffs will show the elements for a prima facie case (very few people of my race have been hired in the last few years). The employer will offer up the affirmative action plan as a legitimate non-discriminatory reason (which sort of doesn't make sense since it is considering race) or offer the affirmative action plan as an alternative to explain the disparity. Then the plaintiff(s) have the burden of proving that the affirmative action plan is invalid by proving that it does not meet the *Weber* test. This may seem like the inverse of what you would expect but it is what the courts require.

To summarize:

There are two methods to prove a systemic disparate treatment claim: facially discriminatory policy or a pattern or practice claim. The BFOQ is the primary statutory defense but the employer may offer some other explanation for a lack of employees in the protected class. The concept of avoiding one type of discrimination with another falls within this type of claim as does voluntary affirmative action plans. Of course, to assert these defenses, they must meet separate tests set forth by the Court.

CHAPTER 5

Systemic Disparate Impact

In the previous two Chapters, the claims at issue required a showing of intent—intent to treat the employee or applicant differently because of their sex or race, etc. What about when there isn't intent but the employer has some policy or test that is keeping out a large number of people in a protected class? The clearest example is height. If an employer has a requirement that all employees must be at least 5'10", this would keep out more women than men. A challenge to this type of policy is a disparate impact claim. Basically, an employer's facially neutral policies affect a protected class more than others and cannot be adequately justified.

The Supreme Court first discussed this claim in Griggs v. Duke Power, 401 U.S. 424 (1971). There the employer had adopted a high school diploma requirement and the Wonderlic test[1] (to be implemented on the very same date that Title VII became effective, hmmmmm). Due to the years of segregated education in North Carolina (the location of the plant), these requirements kept a high

1 Yes, the same one that the NFL gives players during the draft.

number of Black employees from obtaining jobs. The employer couldn't justify the diploma requirement and test as necessary to succeed on the job. Therefore, the Court found that this was a violation of Title VII in that Title VII prohibits "built in headwinds" to equal employment.

After some twists and turns with the Supreme Court easing the burdens on defendants and tightening restrictions on the plaintiff's case, Congress amended Title VII in 1991 (yes, lots of amendments in that 1991 Act) to explicitly include disparate impact in the statute. The ADA has explicit statutory language allowing for disparate impact claims and the Court has interpreted the ADEA to allow such claims. Smith v. City of Jackson, 544 U.S. 228 (2005). Just as with the McDonnell framework, there is a burden shifting scheme.

A. Prima Face Case

It begins, as always, with the plaintiff proving the prima facie case. After proving her membership in a class protected under the statute, the plaintiff must then identify a "Particular Employment Practice." This is whatever facially neutral practice is causing the protected class to lose out. The practice could be a test (physical or written), a height or weight requirement, even a decision by the employer to make promotion decisions based on the subjective judgment of supervisors. Basically, the plaintiff has to point to the specific requirement that is the barrier.[2]

Next, the plaintiff must prove causation—that the employer's use of the practice is causing the impact at the workplace. Finally, the plaintiff must prove that there is a disproportionate impact. Of

---

[2] There is one exception, known as—are you ready—"multicomponent system incapable of separation for purposes of analysis." Whaaaa? This means if the employer uses many different tests and the plaintiff can't tell which test is causing the problem (usually because the employer doesn't keep records), then the plaintiff can point to the "bottom line" of which employees obtain the jobs.

course, the statute doesn't define what counts as "disproportionate." But the EEOC has offered some guidance known as the 80% or 4/5 rule. If the protected group pass rate is less than eighty percent of the non-protected remainder's pass rate, it will be regarded as evidence of adverse impact. Perhaps an example will help:

> Men and women take a test. Of the men, 75% pass; of the women, 25% pass. You are comparing the pass rates. So the protected class, women, pass at a rate of 33% of the men's pass rate. Under the EEOC's rule, this would be evidence of disparate impact.

Even with an understanding of the quantum of impact needed, that doesn't answer the question of the comparison groups to use. If we use a height requirement (employees must be 5'8") as an example, are we comparing the heights of men and women nationally? State-wide? People who actually applied for the job? The Court hasn't been completely consistent. On occasion, the Court has required the impact to fall on actual applicants but in other cases, the Court has found the plaintiffs meet the prima facie case with national statistics.

B. Defendant's Response

As always, the employer may challenge the facts underlying the prima facie case. However, the more common scenario is that the employer asserts a statutory defense. For Title VII, the main defense is known as business necessity and job relatedness. The employer has a burden of proof to show that the requirement is related to the job in question and is tied to measuring successful performance on the job. This is different from the legitimate non-discriminatory reason in the individual disparate treatment framework because it must be *related to the job*. In that way it is similar to the BFOQ from the systemic disparate treatment framework.[3] Because the employer has the burden of proof, the employer can't simply state that the requirement is job related and business necessity.

Instead, courts describe the business necessity defense as requiring the employment policy at issue to measure accurately successful performance on the job. But requirement doesn't have to measure job success perfectly. So, if the employer has a requirement that employees must be 5′10″, then the employer has to prove that being 5′10″ will, in the typical case, set the employee up to be successful on the job.

As with Title VII, under the ADA, the employer must show that qualifications that screen out individuals with disabilities are job related and business necessity. Under the ADEA, however, the employer has a different defense. The Age Discrimination in Employment Act allows for the employer to act based on "reasonable factors other than age." In Meacham v. Knolls Atomic Power Laboratory, 554 U.S. 84 (2008), the Court held this RFOA defense is the correct defense for a disparate claim based on age and further held the employer has the burden of proof to prove the RFOA. This is easier to meet than the business necessity defense—the employment practice just has to be reasonable, not one of business necessity.

C. Section 703(h) Exceptions

There is another set of statutory defenses. Section 703(h) covers certain tests, seniority systems and something known as a piecework system. If the disparity is caused by one of these employment devices, then the employer is not liable.

---

[3] However, the business necessity defense is easier to show because it does not need to be essential to the business.

First, professionally developed tests. There is a LOT of caselaw around the requirements for tests to meet 703(h) which would not be short and happy to discuss. Basically, as long as the test measures something job-related and is not used with the intent to discriminate, and it's an actual professionally developed test (not some idea from Wanda in HR—yes, her again), then the employer hasn't violated the statute by using the test.

Second, bona fide seniority systems are exempt from challenge under disparate impact (again, as long as the employer isn't using a seniority system to discriminate). This means that a system that results in different compensation or benefits to different groups of employees is allowed.

Third, 703(h) allows an employer to pay people by the quantity of their work or the quality of their work. In other words, if the employer is paying by the number of bushels of beans you pick, even if this causes a disparate impact, there isn't a violation of Title VII.[4]

D. Plaintiff's Rebuttal

If the plaintiff is able to prove the prima facie case and the employer proves business necessity and job relatedness, the plaintiff has one last chance to show a violation. This is the "alternative employment practice" stage. Here, the plaintiff is trying to offer some other way to meet the employer's goals without having the disparate impact. In addition, the plaintiff has to show that it is reasonable to expect the employer to use this "alternative device." This means that the plaintiff has to show that the new practice won't be excessively costly.

4 This is known as a bona fide merit and piecework system.

To summarize:

Plaintiff proves:

Protected class

Specific neutral practice

Causes

Disproportionate impact

Employer proves:

Business necessity and job relatedness

703(h) defense

Or RFOA for an age claim

Plaintiff proves:

Alternative employment practice

BUT WAIT!

Now that you have learned all about disparate impact claims, let me bring another recent Executive Order to your attention. In 2025, President Trump signed an executive order declaring that "[i]t is the policy of the United States to eliminate the use of disparate-impact liability in all contexts to the maximum degree possible to avoid violating the Constitution, Federal civil rights laws, and basic American ideals." Further, the order requires all agencies to "deprioritize enforcement of all statutes and regulations to the extent they include disparate-impact liability."

Regardless of this order, disparate impact remains a statutorily available claim and private plaintiffs may litigate on a disparate impact claim.

Read on for a quick note comparing the three main frameworks and some advice on how to choose a framework!

CHAPTER 6

Pulling It All Together

A Quick Note on the Three Frameworks

Now you know all about the three main frameworks! Students usually find it helpful to compare them against each other. Great news! I did that for you.

Individual Disparate Treatment (single motive)	Individual Disparate Treatment (mixed motive)	Systemic Disparate Treatment	Disparate Impact
Plaintiff *(burden of persuasion)* PFC: • Protected class • Adverse Action • Qualified • Applied for Open position	**Plaintiff** *(burden of persuasion)* PFC: • Protected class • Adverse Action	**Plaintiff** *(burden of persuasion)* PFC: • Facially discriminatory policy OR • Standard operating procedure to discriminate	**Plaintiff** *(burden of persuasion)* PFC: • Protected class • Specific Employment (neutral) practice • Causes

• Circumstances giving rise to inference of discrimination	• Protected class is motivating factor in adverse action	against the class	• Disproportionate Impact on protected class
Defendant *(burden of production)* LNDR	**Defendant** *(burden of persuasion)* Same decision defense	**Defendant** • BFOQ *(burden of persuasion)* • Alternative explanation • Affirmative action plan	**Defendant** *(burden of persuasion)* • Business Necessity • 703(h) defenses • Reasonable factors other than age (for an ADEA claim)
Plaintiff *(burden of persuasion)* Pretext	Ø	**Plaintiff** *(burden of persuasion)* No burden shift unless affirmative action plan. Then plaintiff must show plan does not meet the *Weber* test.	**Plaintiff** *(burden of persuasion)* Alternative Employment Practice

Let's also consider the defenses side-by-side. In order of easiest for the defendant to meet to hardest:

Legitimate, non-discriminatory reason (could be anything, burden of production)

Reasonable factor other than age (ADEA only; burden of proof, has to be reasonable)

Business Necessity and Job related (burden of proof)

Bona Fide Occupational Qualification (burden of proof, has to go to the essence of the business)

Finally, students are often flummoxed by which framework should be used in different factual scenarios. Although this is very, very (very) basic, use this handy flow chart to get yourself started.

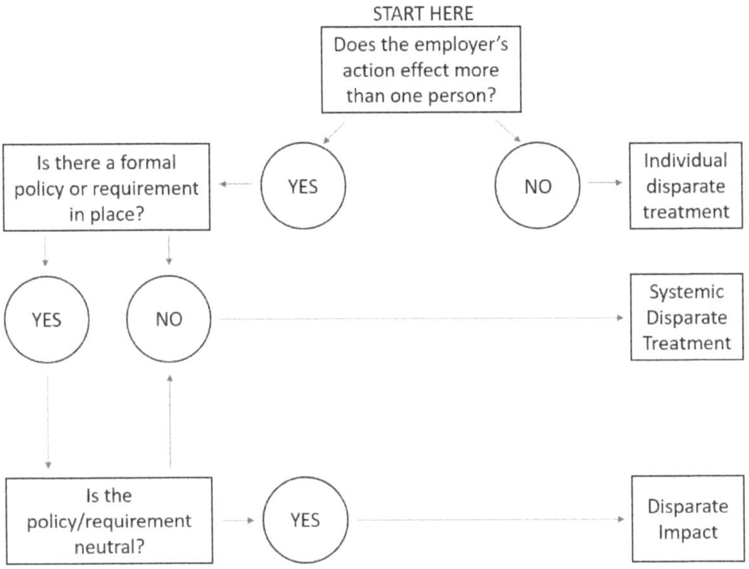

CHAPTER 7

Retaliation

Imagine you have told your boss that you are being harassed by Betty, a co-worker. Your boss responds "What? I can't believe that you would accuse Betty of harassment! You're fired!" The next employee that Betty harasses would be much less likely to come forward and complain. To keep this from happening (ideally), the Big Three statutes all prohibit retaliation either with explicit language or through judicial interpretation.

The language is similar across the three statutes:

> It shall be an unlawful employment practice for an employer to discriminate against any of his employees or applicants for employment because he has opposed any practice made an unlawful employment practice by this title, or because he has made a charge, testified, assisted, or participated in any manner in an investigation, proceeding, or hearing under this title.[1]

Whew! That's a mouthful! Fortunately, this is a very straightforward claim—at least framework-wise.

1 42 U.S.C. § 2000e-3.

A. Who May Sue

What if an employee files a charge of discrimination and the employer retaliates by firing her fiancé (who works at the same location)? The person who filed the charge hasn't been injured and the person who was fired didn't engage in any type of protected conduct (more on that below). This is the exact fact pattern in Thompson v. North American Stainless, LP, 562 U.S. 170 (2011). There, the Court held that Thompson fell within the "zone of interests" sought to be protected by the statute and should be considered an aggrieved individual. Therefore, he could bring a retaliation claim.[2] So, anyone within the "zone of interests" may bring a claim if they suffer an adverse action.

B. Framework

Good ol' *McDonnell Douglas,* single motive, burden shifting applies to a retaliation claim. It's the basic prima facie case, then a legitimate non-discriminatory reason produced by the defendant and finishing up with a showing of pretext by the plaintiff. Of course, the elements of the prima face case are different!

1. Prima Facie Case

There are three elements to the prima facie case: the plaintiff engaged in protected conduct; there is an adverse employment action; and the protected conduct caused the adverse employment action.

---

[2] The Court didn't give a lot of detail as to who may bring a claim under this "zone of interests" test: a family member fired will meet the test and a mere acquaintance slapped on the wrist will not.

a) Protected Conduct

There are two types of protected conduct: opposition and participation. It is important to determine which type of conduct is at issue because they receive different levels of protection.

Opposition conduct involves actions NOT part of an official proceeding (in court or a before an agency) where the employee is explicitly challenging, opposing, or questioning an employment practice by the employer. For example, internal complaints, union grievances, or media statements would be considered "opposition" conduct. In Crawford v. Metro Gov't of Nashville, 555 U.S. 271 (2009), the Court made clear that the "opposition" conduct doesn't have to be at the plaintiff's initiative. In other words, if during an investigation, the employee is asked if she was harassed and she says yes, that counts as protected opposition conduct.

The employee has to be opposing something unlawful under the statute to in order to be bring an opposition claim under the statute. In other words, you don't have a retaliation claim under Title VII unless you were opposing something that is a violation of Title VII. But, the employer conduct you are opposing doesn't have to be ACTUALLY unlawful. You just need a reasonable belief that the action is unlawful. Clark County v. Breeden, 532 U.S. 268 (2001).

Finally, the form the opposition conduct takes has to be reasonable. You can't burn down the workplace to protest to discriminatory hiring practices and expect to be protected. Clandestine sneaky information gathering is another example of conduct that doesn't get protection. For example, when an employee copies confidential information and sends the information to someone else, this is unprotected conduct.

Participation conduct is conduct within some kind of official action, either with an agency or a court. It can be something less than the filing a lawsuit. For example, participation covers testimony at trial or in discovery. Gathering information for pending litigation will be considered participation (unless it's the sneaky stuff). But a threat to file a claim without carrying through wouldn't be considered participation conduct but would be considered opposition conduct.

Participation conduct gets almost absolute protection. I say "almost" because some courts have refused protection to conduct that is in bad faith or false. Unlike opposition conduct, participation conduct doesn't require a reasonable belief that the employer action is unlawful.

b) Adverse Employment Action

The Court set the standard for what counts as an adverse employment action in Burlington Northern & Santa Fe v. White, 548 U.S. 53 (2006). The retaliation itself—the adverse action—doesn't have to take place in workplace. It must be some action by the employer that is materially adverse and would have dissuade a reasonable worker from making or supporting a charge of discrimination. So taking away the cookies in the break room won't count but taking away the ability to take every other Friday off would count.

c) Causation

The employee has to prove that the protected conduct caused the adverse action. Of course, that means the plaintiff will have to prove that employer was aware of the protected conduct.[3] The causation must be but for causation. No mixed motive retaliation claims! Univ. of Texas Southwestern Medical Center v. Nassar, 570 U.S. 338 (2013).

---

[3] Some courts list "employer knowledge" as a separate element of the prima facie case.

2. *Legitimate Non-discriminatory Reason*

Nothing tricky here! The employer will produce some legitimate non-discriminatory reason for the adverse action. "Your transfer has nothing to do with that letter to editor you sent about our hiring practices! We had already planned to transfer you."

3. *Pretext*

The burden then shifts to the plaintiff to show that the defendant's LNDR was truly pretextual for the defendant's actual discriminatory motive. Just as with an individual disparate treatment claim, the plaintiff may prove pretext with direct evidence ("That's it! You complained about Betty—off to Siberia with you!") or circumstantial evidence. A common method for circumstantial evidence is what's referred to as "temporal proximity" which just means that the protected conduct and the adverse action happened close in time. In many retaliation cases, this is all the evidence the plaintiff has to prove retaliatory intent. In shocking news to zero law students, the courts are split on how close in time the actions must be but a few months will generally suffice to establish the inference.

Otherwise, that's it for pretext. No mixed motive claims![4]

To summarize:

PFC

- Protected Conduct
  - Opposition or Participation
- Adverse Employment Action
- Causation

---

[4] There is also no such thing as a disparate impact retaliation claim. You must prove the retaliatory intent.

LNDR

PRETEXT (no mixed motive)

CHAPTER 8

Equal Pay Act of 1963[1]

The Equal Pay Act is another statute that covers compensation in the workplace. The EPA is an amendment to the Fair Labor Standards Act (which deals with wages and hours). It covers only *wages* and only prohibits discrimination on the basis of sex.[2]

Unlike Title VII, ADA, and the ADEA, the Equal Pay Act does not define the covered employer by a minimum number of employees. Instead, it covers employees who are engaged in interstate commerce or in production of goods for interstate commerce. Employees are also covered if they work for an "enterprise" engaged in interstate commerce or production of goods for interstate commerce, with two or more EEs and generates a particular minimum amount of revenue. State, local and federal workers are all covered. Unions are also covered—they are prohibited from trying to have the employer violate the EPA.

What does the EPA prohibit? It prohibits the employer from paying wages to employees at a rate less than the rate paid to

---

1 26 U.S.C. 206(d).

2 Technically it covers the "rate" of pay which means the statute covers wages but also bonuses, vacation pay, etc.

employees "of the opposite sex"[3] for "equal work." What counts as "equal work"? Excellent question! The statute goes on to define "equal work" as "the performance of which requires equal skill, effort, and responsibility, and which are performed under similar working conditions."

A. The Prima Facie Case

The prima facie case is very straight forward:

1) Unequal wages paid

2) Equal work performed

3) On the basis of sex

A plaintiff isn't required to prove intent. But a plaintiff does have to prove she[4] is performing equal work to the employee of the opposite sex (this person is known as the "comparator.") Again, equal work means the jobs require equal skill, effort, and responsibility. In Corning Glass Works v. Brennan, 417 U.S. 188 (1974), the Court held that the jobs don't have to be identical. Instead, the jobs should be substantially equal. As for the requirement that the jobs are performed under "similar working conditions," the Court interpreted that language to mean "substantially similar."

When comparing the jobs at issue, the focus is on the *actual job requirements*. Attempted shenanigans like different job titles or job descriptions won't protect an employer if the job are indeed the same. As mentioned above, a plaintiff needs to pick out a "comparator"—an employee of the opposite sex performing "equal work" who is being paid more. This could be tricky in a sex

---

[3] Very binary, right?

[4] The Act covers male employees paid less than female employees as well.

segregated workplace.[5] But the comparator employee could be a former employee (or even a subsequent employee in the same job).

B. Defenses

Once the plaintiff proves these elements, the burden shifts to the employer to prove one of the statutory defenses. Whatever reason is offered, it must, actually, explain the disparity in wages.

- Seniority system; this defense is met as long as the system meets the requirements under Title VII.
- Merit system: this applies to objective measurements of job performance
- Incentive system: this applies to a measured output system by quality or quantity
- Other factor other than sex: this is the main defense![6]

As you can imagine, most of the litigation focuses on what counts as a factor other than sex. Courts have rejected a few arguments. First, if an employer had previously set salaries based on sex and NOW sets salaries based on its past salaries, then past pay doesn't amount to a factor other than sex. Second, if an employer is paying women less than men simply because women are willing to work for less than men (i.e. a market forces argument), courts have rejected that argument. But economic profitability has been accepted. In other words, if one section of the workplace earns more revenue, then paying employees in that section a higher wage is a "factor other than sex."

---

5 The EPA applies to employees working in the same "establishment" which leads to questions about how to define "establishment." For example, in a chain restaurant, each restaurant would be considered a different establishment.

6 An argument can be made that showing that a factor other than sex is the reason for the pay disparity means that the plaintiff can't prove the prima facie case. However, the statute treats this as an affirmative defense and therefore places the burden of proof on the employer.

If an employer pays a woman less than a man working in the same job because his prior salary was higher, is this a factor other sex? Courts had (HAD, I said) been unified in allowing prior salary to meet the factor other than sex. But recently, at least one Circuit court has rejected prior salary as a factor other than sex in all fact situations. Rather, the employer must show that prior salary is somehow job-related. Stay tuned for how this develops!

If an employer cannot prove one of the affirmative defenses, then the employer must raise the wage of the underpaid employee (as opposed to dropping the wage of the higher paid employee). In addition, the successful employee is entitled to back pay and liquidated damages.[7]

C. Interaction with Title VII

Because Title does cover terms and conditions of employment, compensation claims may be brought under Title VII. A plaintiff will have to choose one of the frameworks discussed in Chapters 3-5. Because Title VII doesn't have an equal work requirement and doesn't have the "same establishment" requirement, the Court held in County of Washington v. Gunther, 452 U.S. 161 (1981), that the proof requirements of EPA actions do NOT apply to sex-based wage claims. In other words, a plaintiff bringing a sex-based wage claims doesn't have to meet the "equal work" standards. Even if the jobs are not equal, if the plaintiff is able to prove an intent to pay her less because of her sex, then there is a violation of Title VII. Courts are split as to whether a challenge requires a facially discriminatory system or whether a plaintiff can prove a violation through the *McDonnell Douglas* framework.

But (there's always a "but"), in a piece of legislation known as the Bennett Amendment, Congress incorporated the Equal Pay Act

---

[7] Check out Chapter 13.

defenses into Title VII. In other words, if the wages paid wouldn't violate the EPA, then the wages don't violate Title VII. The Court held that all four defenses from EPA are incorporated into Title VII. Keep in mind that "factor other than sex" is an easier defense to prove than job relatedness and business necessity.

D. Comparable Worth

One last note. Comparable worth is the theory that jobs that are of the same value to the employer should be paid the same, even if it isn't the same job or an "equal job." An often-used example is comparing administrative assistants to custodians. One could argue that these jobs are of comparable worth to the employer and should be paid the same. However compelling you may or may not find this theory to be, courts have rejected it under both Title VII and the Equal Pay Act.

CHAPTER 9

Protected Classes Under Title VII: Some Twists and Turns and a Few More Frameworks

In this Chapter, we will discuss some special issues for the protected classes of Title VII. Let's approach this one protected class at a time.

A. Race and Color

Perhaps somewhat surprisingly, there isn't much to discuss for the protected classes of race and color under Title VII. Remember that Title VII isn't limited to claims of discrimination by BIPOC. A White employee may claim race discrimination.

The definition of race is fairly broad and could include Middle Eastern or Pacific Islander, for example. Color means just that—the color of one's skin. This isn't a commonly litigated claim but has been brought when an employer favors dark-skinned Black employees over light-skinned (or vice versa).

One quirk to race discrimination to keep in mind is that refusing to hire an applicant because of the race of his spouse is unlawful race discrimination under the statute.

Finally, remember: NO RACE BASED BFOQ!

B. Religion

This protected class is more complicated! There are a few different issues under religion: exemptions; a duty to accommodate religious practices; and, the ministerial exception. Exemptions, exceptions, sounds confusing? Never fear—your short and happy explanation is ahead!

Before we dive into all of that, let's set out the definition of religion or religious belief. Title VII doesn't define "religious belief" (this will become a theme in this Chapter). However, courts have concluded that religious beliefs include not only majoritarian religions but theistic beliefs and moral and ethical beliefs that assume the place of religious beliefs. Circular, right? A claim for discrimination because of religion could be also based upon an applicant's atheist beliefs.

Also keep in mind that an individual's religious beliefs might not be apparent. In order to prove that the employer was discriminating because of religion, a plaintiff may need to prove that the employer knew of her religious beliefs. However, in EEOC v. Abercrombie & Fitch, 575 U.S. 768 (2015), the Court held that the employer's motivation, rather than knowledge, is the important factor. In other words, the employer might be motivated by its belief that the employee has a particular religious belief even if the employer has no direct knowledge of the belief.

1. Exemptions

Religious employers are exempt from the prohibition of discrimination on the basis of religion. Specifically, Title VII states:

> This title shall not apply to a religious corporation, association, educational institution, or society with respect to the employment of individuals of a particular religion to perform work connected with carrying on the activities of such an entity.[1]

There is also an exemption for educational institutions employing people "of a particular religion."[2] These exemptions allow religious employers to employ people of a particular religion. In other words, the exemption applies *only* to discrimination because of religion. The exemption does not allow a religious institution to discriminate because of race or sex. (See below for discussion of the ministerial exception).

2. Duty to Accommodate

Title VII places an affirmative obligation on employers to accommodate the religious practices and observances of its employees. The employer must do so unless there is an undue hardship.[3]

Traditionally the framework for proving a failure to accommodate claim was as follows:

Plaintiff proves:

1) he has a religious practice or belief

2) that conflicts with an employment requirement

---

1 42 U.S.C. § 2000e-1(a).

2 42 U.S.C. § 2000e-2(e).

3 42 U.S.C. § 2000e-1(j).

3) the employee requested an accommodation

4) and the employer refused the accommodation.

Employer then proves either:

1) it made a reasonable accommodation OR

2) it cannot provide a reasonable accommodation because of an undue hardship.

That said, in the *Abercrombie* case mentioned above, the Court seemed to create one unified theory for religious discrimination. Refusing an accommodation, in this view, is simply a type of discrimination because of religion. The lower courts haven't completely abandoned the traditional framework and are still sorting this out.

Turning to the obligation to reasonably accommodate, the employer must provide some manner of change in the workplace to allow the employee to engage in his religious practice. For example, an exception from the "no caps" rule for an employee who wears a head scarf. Or allowing an employee to take breaks at a certain time to engage in prayer.

To meet this obligation, an employer does not need to select the reasonable accommodation suggested by the employee. In addition, the employer doesn't to prove that the accommodation suggested by the employee would create an undue hardship. As long as the accommodation offered allows the employee to engage in her observance or practice, then the employer has met its obligation. Ansonia Board of Education v. Philbrook, 479 U.S. 60 (1986).

An employer needs to prove undue hardship only if it is going to argue that it can't provide any reasonable accommodation. There isn't a definition in the statute of "undue hardship" (see, I told you it would be a theme). In 2023, for the first time in almost 40 years, the Court addressed the test for "undue hardship." Previously, the

Court had held that anything more than a de minimis cost on the employer would meet the undue hardship threshold. TWA v. Hardison, 432 U.S. 63 (1977). In Groff v. DeJoy, 600 U.S. 447 (2023), the Court raised the threshold, holding that an undue hardship will be found only if there is a "substantial" increased cost in relation to the conduct of the employer's business. The Court further made clear that this standard is more exacting standard than the previous de minimis standard. Further, an undue hardship cannot be established simply on the basis of co-worker reaction to religion in the workplace. In essence, the Court raised the burden for employers to show that they cannot provide an accommodation to an employee's religious practices.

3. *Ministerial Exception*

Remember that the statutory exemption applies only to discrimination because of religion. Under the terms of the statute, an employee could sue a religious organization for discrimination under any of the other protected classes of Title VII or under the ADEA or the ADA. Not so fast!

It is now well established that the courts may not hear any discrimination claims if the employee in question falls within the "ministerial exception." Although lower courts had long employed the doctrine, the Supreme Court first adopted it in 2012 in Hosanna-Tabor Evangelical Lutheran Church v. EEOC, 565 U.S. 171 (2012). This doctrine holds that if the employee in question is a "minister,"[4] an action would interfere with the Free Exercise rights of the religious organization to hear a discrimination claim. In other words, who is the court to tell a church who should and shouldn't be a minister?

---

[4] This is defined more broadly than Christian religions who use the term "minister."

Example: A female minister alleges that she was discriminated against on the basis of sex when she was removed from her position after her pregnancy. The court would dismiss the claim because it would require the court to determine matters of internal church doctrine.

The *existence* of the ministerial exception is well-settled. The *definition* is more of a cutting edge issue. In *Hosanna-Tabor,* the Court looked to factors such as the formal title of the employee, the substance reflected in the title, the employee's own use of the title, and the important religious functions performed by the employee. Applying this test, the Court found that a "called" teacher at religious school who taught religious education and held the title of Minister was within this exception. Therefore, the Court dismissed her claim under the Americans with Disabilities Act.

In 2020, the Court returned to the question of the contours of the ministerial exception and broadened the scope of the exception. In Our Lady of Guadalupe School v. Morrisey-Berru, 591 U.S. 732 (2020), the Court downplayed the importance of the factors discussed in *Hosanna-Tabor*. Instead, when considering the claims (one of age discrimination and the other under the ADA) of two teachers at religious schools, the Court held it is the actual duties of the job that determine whether an employee is within the exception. "What matters, at bottom, is what an employee does." Because the teachers were involved in educating students in the Catholic faith and inculcating Catholic teachings, the teachers were within the ministerial exception. Therefore, the discrimination claims could not be heard by the courts.

C. National Origin

The term "national origin" is—say it with me—not defined in Title VII. Courts have defined this protected class to include an individual's ancestry, not citizenship. In other words, national origin refers to the country you or your ancestors came from. Espinoza v. Farah Mfg., 414 U.S. 86 (1973). So refusing to hire someone because they are not a U.S. citizen is not national origin discrimination. Further, not hiring someone because she is from Philadelphia or Georgia is *not* national origin discrimination (but refusing to hire someone because he is Puerto Rican would be).

When considering national origin discrimination, another statute comes into play. The Immigration Reform and Control Act of 1986[5] mandates that employers not hire someone unauthorized to work in the United States and requires employers to verify eligibility to work. However, IRCA also prohibits discrimination because of national origin or citizenship status. The concern, of course, was that employers would refuse to hire people out of a fear that workers from certain countries were not authorized to work. IRCA tries to counteract this fear by prohibiting national origin discrimination.

One last issue for national origin discrimination involves language and accent rules. The question is whether actions taken on the basis of the language spoken or a foreign accent amount to facial discrimination. If it is facial discrimination, then the employer may defend only with a BFOQ. The courts are split in this area. At very least, discriminating against someone because of their language or foreign accent is evidence of national origin discrimination. In addition, requiring employees to speak English at all times at work (including during breaks) could give rise to a hostile work environment on the basis of national origin.

D. Sex

There are many sub-issues in sex discrimination, including an additional framework or two! Keep in mind that men may bring a

---

[5] 18 U.S.C. § 1324(A).

claim of sex discrimination. Further, the Court in *Price Waterhouse* held that evidence of sex stereotyping is evidence of discrimination because of sex. For example, firing a man because he is not meeting the employer's view of masculinity is discrimination on the basis of stereotypes and therefore discrimination because of sex.

1. Sexual Orientation and Transgender Employees

Until June 2020, the answer to the question "is sexual orientation protected under Title VII" was "no, unless maybe the employee can argue some sort of stereotyping claim under the *Price Waterhouse* decision." However, in Bostock v. Clayton County, 590 U.S. 644 (2020), the Court held that the prohibition of discrimination because of sex covers discrimination because of sexual orientation or transgender status. The reasoning employed by the Court makes clear that *any* discrimination because of sexual orientation or transgender is prohibited by Title VII. In other words, the employee will need not to show any special fact patterns or stereotyping.

Following *Bostock,* the EEOC issued a "technical assistance document" which stated that employers could not deny employees equal access to bathrooms, locker rooms, or showers that correspond to their gender identity. Then in 2024, the EEOC for the first time 30 years updated its enforcement guidance on harassment in the workplace.[6] The EEOC stated that harassment of LGBTQ+ workers is a violation of Title VII.

In shocking news to no one, both the updated enforcement guidance and the technical assistance document were challenged. In one action, 19 states joined together, led by Tennessee and in

[6] By Executive Order, President Trump sought to rescind the EEOC Guidance on Gender Identity. AOTW, the EEOC does have not enough Commissioners to meet the required quorum to take action and therefore, the Guidance remains in place.

another, the State of Texas and a think tank brought the action. In *Texas v. EEOC*, the Northern District of Texas vacated parts of the guidance, finding that they exceeded the EEOC's authority by expanding the definition of "sex" beyond the biological binary and by defining "harassment" to include such actions failure to accommodate dress, pronoun, and bathroom preferences.

The guidance was not withdrawn by the EEOC in the first half of 2025 because the EEOC lacked a quorum of Commissioners. However, it is most likely by the publication of this edition that there will be a quorum and parts of the guidance will be withdrawn (thereby mooting the litigation).[7]

2. Grooming and Dress Codes

Despite the fact that many dress codes or grooming standards have different standards for men and women (and yes, are very binary), such standards do not violate Title VII merely because of those differences. In other words, even though these standards have facial differences based on sex, the courts have consistently held that there is no violation of Title VII.

> Example: Women may have long hair but men must have short hair.[8]
>
> Example: Men may not wear make-up or jewelry.

However, gender specific grooming or dress codes which impose an unequal burden of time or money on one sex are unlawful. The plaintiff will need to have evidence of the cost or time needed to meet the standard.

---

7 In United States v. Skrmetti, 605 U.S. ___, 145 S. Ct. 1816 (2025) (medical care for transgender minors), the Court noted that it has not "considered whether *Bostock*'s reasoning reaches beyond the Title VII context" and it declined to do so.

8 Fun fact: Many of the early grooming standard cases were brought by men with long hair.

> Example: Female employees must wear make-up and nail polish and style, curl, or tease their hair. Male employees must be showered.

3. *Pregnancy*

After the Supreme Court held that pregnancy discrimination was not discrimination because of sex,[9] Congress got into the act and enacted the Pregnancy Discrimination Act of 1978 (PDA). The PDA amended Title VII and added two clauses. The first clause is really just expanding the definition of "sex."

> The term 'because of sex' or 'on the basis of sex' include, but are not limited to, because of or on the basis of pregnancy, childbirth or related medical conditions;[10]
>
> By adding pregnancy to the definition of sex, then any actions because of pregnancy are treated the same as employment actions taken because of sex.
>
> Example: A policy refusing to hire pregnant women would be facially discriminatory and could only be defended with a BFOQ.

The second clause of the PDA created all the confusion:

> women affected by pregnancy, childbirth, or related medical conditions shall be treated the same for all employment-related purposes . . . as other persons not so affected but similar in their ability or inability to work.

Courts read this language to prevent employers from treating pregnancy and related conditions less favorably than other medical conditions. For example, suppose an employer fired a pregnant

---

[9] Because, the Court said, discriminating on the basis of pregnancy is dividing employees into "pregnant" and "not pregnant" isn't purely along the lines of sex. Both groups will include women.

[10] "Related medical conditions" include abortion, in vitro procedures, and most likely breast feeding (although not all courts have found breast feeding to be covered).

woman who required numerous sick days due to morning sickness. If the employer would fire any employee who required numerous sick days, then there is no discrimination because of pregnancy. The pregnant worker is treated the same as all other workers.

4. *Accommodating Pregnant Workers*

First off, let me just tell you that prior to 2022, this section was pretty short! But in keeping with one of our themes, it's not so short anymore. Prior to 2022, there was no obligation under federal statutes for employers to provide accommodations for pregnant workers. If a pregnant worker needs a desk job because she shouldn't stand on her feet, the employer had no obligation to provide this accommodation. Further, pregnant workers are not covered under the Americans with Disabilities Act.

In 2015, the Supreme Court interpreted Title VII to require employers to provide accommodations to pregnant workers in certain circumstances (discussed in more detail below). Then Congress got in on the act and passed legislation, the Pregnant Workers Fairness Act, to require employers to provide accommodations. In keeping with the theme of this edition, litigation has been filed to challenge both the legislation and the implementing regulations. Given that the PWFA might be overturned by the time you read this, both the PWFA and the Court's decision are discussed here.

To begin—the Pregnant Workers Fairness Act.[11] The PWFA only applies to accommodations and does not replace laws that are more protective of pregnant workers. Covered employers are private and public sector employers with at least 15 employees, Congress, federal agencies, employment agencies, and labor organizations.

---

[11] 42 U.S.C. § 2000gg.

Under the PWFA, employers must provide reasonable accommodations to a pregnant employee or applicant for known limitations related to pregnancy, childbirth or related medical conditions unless doing so would lead to an undue hardship for the employer. Undue hardship is defined as significant difficulty or expense.

What type of accommodations might an employer provide? Well, imagine you are pregnant at work—what might you need to continue your employment? How about uniforms and safety apparel that fits, light duty assignments, additional break time to use the bathroom (trust me, this is key), the ability to sit while working, and perhaps closer parking.

In addition to requiring the provision of accommodations, covered employers are prohibited from requiring a covered employee to accept an accommodation other than any reasonable accommodation arrived at through the interactive process or to take leave, whether paid or unpaid, if another reasonable accommodation can be provided. Employers also may not deny employment opportunities to a qualified employee if such denial is based on the need to make reasonable accommodations or take adverse action in terms, conditions, or privileges of employment against a qualified employee on account of the employee requesting or using a reasonable accommodation.

Finally, as with all anti-discrimination statutes, employers are prohibited from retaliating against an employee for exercising their rights under the statute.

That's the statute itself. The EEOC issued a Final Rule implementing the PWFA in April 2024. Among other things, the Rule further defined "related medical conditions" that must be accommodated to include miscarriage, stillbirth, or abortion. Further, the Rule does not include a blanket religious exemption.

The final rule has been challenged in several lawsuits by a number of states and Catholic organizations on a wide variety of grounds, including the First Amendment, the Administrative Procedures Act, the lack of a religious exemption, the Religious Freedom Restoration Act. Injunctions, both preliminary and permanent, have been issued against different aspects of the Rule, primarily the requirement that accommodations be provided to employees seeking abortions or infertility treatments. A nationwide injunction was issued in May 2025 against a requirement that employers accommodate elective abortions which are not medically necessary.[12]

Apart from the Rule, the PWFA itself has been challenged as invalid. During the pandemic, the House of Representatives adopted a Rule whereby members could by proxy (as opposed to in-person). The PWFA was enacted under this Rule with 226 of 431 members of the House voting by proxy. The State of Texas challenged the proxy rule as unconstitutional under the Quorum Clause and argued therefore the PWFA was not properly enacted. The Northern District of Texas upheld the State's argument. So, the PWFA cannot be enforced against the State of Texas acting as an employer. The case is, AOTW, on appeal. Now, I know, this seems very specific to include in a purported short and happy guide! But this claim seems like a roadmap to other states who wish to challenge the PWFA, doesn't it?

Given all of this litigation and injunctions and whatnot, it's important to understand the Supreme Court decision that preceded all this. If the PWFA is overturned, the Court's decision in Young v. UPS, 575 U.S. 206 (2015) will govern. The decision is still good law but because the PWFA is more favorable to pregnant workers, most employees will look to the statute first.

---

[12] Honestly, by the time I finished typing this footnote, something new will have happened.

In *Young v. UPS*, the plaintiff was a pregnant driver. Her doctor placed her under a lifting restriction. When she asked UPS for an accommodation, UPS refused and told her that she couldn't work until the lifting restriction was no longer in place. However, UPS did accommodate other workers with limitations. The Court set out a burden-shifting framework for failure to accommodate pregnancy claims. This framework applies ONLY when there is an accommodation (like light duty assignment) which has been offered to some employees but not pregnant employees.

The Court says it is applying the *McDonnell Douglas* framework. We'll see . . .

Plaintiff proves the prima facie case:

1) membership in protected class [pregnant]

2) sought accommodation [may I please have a light duty assignment?]

3) employer refused accommodation [no]

4) employer accommodated others similar in their ability or inability to work [employees injured on the job are accommodated]

Employer produces as a legitimate non-discriminatory reason.

The Court stated that the LNDR can *not* be that accommodating pregnancy is more expensive.

Plaintiff then proves pretext.

This all sounds very *McDonnell Douglas*-y up to this point. It goes off the rails when the Court explains "pretext" in this scenario. The Court said the plaintiff may prove pretext by proving that the failure to accommodate is a significant burden on pregnant workers and the legitimate non-discriminatory reason offered is not sufficiently strong to justify the burden. Therefore, an inference of discrimination is present.

Remember, this framework *only* applies to issues of accommodation and *only* if other workers are accommodated.

One other issue in the area of accommodation involves *more* accommodation for pregnant workers. The Supreme Court found that a state law that requires employers to provide leave for pregnant workers (and not other workers) is not preempted by Title VII. Cal. Fed. Savings & Loan Assoc. v. Guerra, 479 U.S. 272 (1987). Make sure to keep in mind that the PDA applies to pregnancy, not child-rearing! If the employer grants parental leave (as opposed to disability leave for pregnancy), it needs to do so equally between men and women.

Another piece of legislation relevant to this area is the Providing Urgent Medical Protections for Nursing Mothers Act (PUMP) Act, effective April 2023. The PUMP Act requires employers of all sizes to provide a reasonable break for employees to express breast milk, with a private area out of view and without intrusion (not the bathroom) to pump.[13] The Act requires the employee to notify the employer of a failure to provide a private space and to allow the employer ten days to comply. For other violations, there is no notice requirement. The PUMP Act has not faced the same challenges as the PWFA and litigation has focused on the notice requirements.

5. *Harassment*

Each of the Big Three statutes prohibits discrimination in "terms, conditions or privileges of employment." Courts interpreted this language to prohibit conduct when it alters terms and conditions of employment because of the employee's sex, race, age, disability status, etc. Harassment claims fall into two categories: with a tangible employment action (known as quid pro quo) and without a tangible employment action (known as a hostile

[13] Employers with fewer than 50 employees may raise an undue hardship defense, requiring a showing of significant difficulty or expense.

environment claim). A hostile environment claim might be created because of any protected class. However, a quid pro quo claim can only be based on sex.

Whether a claim should be considered a hostile environment claim or a quid pro quo depends entirely on whether there is a tangible employment action at issue. The Court gave us a list of the type of employment decisions that count as tangible employment actions:

- hiring,
- firing,
- failing to promote,
- reassignment with significantly different responsibilities, or
- a decision causing a significant change in benefits.

If one of the above actions is conditioned on sexual conduct, then the claim is a quid pro quo claim. If it isn't conditioned on sexual conduct, then it is a hostile environment claim.

a) Quid Pro Quo

In legalese, a quid pro quo claim exists when sexual conduct is condition of tangible employment benefits, including salary, promotion, and continued employment. In every day terms, there's a quid pro quo claim when a supervisor says "have sex with me or I'll fire you." If the employee agrees in order to keep her job, or if she refuses and then is fired, there is an actionable quid pro quo claim. If the employee says "get lost,"[14] and isn't fired, there is no actionable quid pro quo (although there might be a hostile environment claim).

---

[14] Feel free to use your imagination to fill in other statements.

This isn't a burden shifting scheme. The plaintiff has to prove: 1) a supervisor 2) conditioned a tangible employment action on 3) submission to sexual conduct. There's no burden shift or defenses. If the plaintiff proves the three elements, the employer is liable.

b) Hostile Work Environment

First recognized by the Supreme Court in Meritor v. Vinson, 477 U.S. 57 (1986), a hostile environment claim applies in situations where there hasn't been a tangible employment action but the workplace is abusive or hostile because of the plaintiff's membership in a protected class. In other words, if the boss or co-workers comment all day about the employee's physical appearance or physically grab the employee, there is a hostile environment claim.

The plaintiff must prove:

1) The conduct was because of the protected class;[15]

2) The conduct was unwelcome;

   This applies ONLY in cases of hostile environment based on sex. "Unwelcome" does not mean the activity was under duress. Instead, it means uninvited.

3) The conduct was severe or pervasive;

   Because this element asks if the conduct is severe OR pervasive, there might be an actionable claim based on one incident if the incident is severe enough (for example, a physical assault). In Harris v. Forklift Systems, Inc., 510 U.S. 17 (1993), the Court

---

[15] A hostile environment claim may be present even if the harasser and the harassee are in the same protected class. For example, in Oncale v. Sundowner Offshore Servs., Inc., 523 U.S. 75 (1998), the Court held that same-sex harassment may be actionable as long as the other elements of the claim are met.

provided a few factors to help determine if the conduct is severe or pervasive.

- Severity of the discriminatory conduct
- Frequency of the discriminatory conduct
- Whether the conduct is physically threatening/humiliating
- Whether it unreasonably interferes with your work performance.

4) The conduct altered the work environment both objectively and subjectively;

The plaintiff must find the conduct to be hostile and a reasonable person must find the conduct to be hostile and change the work environment. The plaintiff doesn't need to have a mental breakdown but does need to find the environment abusive or hostile.

5) Employer Liability.

Remember that the statutes place liability on the employer, not the harasser. Employer liability depends on the organizational status of the harasser(s). We can separate harassers into two broad categories: supervisors and co-workers (which may also include customers or clients). What's needed here is a chart!

	Supervisor	Co-workers
Tangible employment action (aka	Liability (yup, that's it. If the employee proves the elements, there's liability.)	Doesn't exist. Co-workers cannot take tangible employment

quid pro quo)		actions against co-workers.
No tangible employment action (aka hostile environment)	Vicarious liability with an affirmative defense: (a) it used reasonable care to prevent[16] and promptly correct harassment AND (b) the employee unreasonably failed to use reporting procedures created by the employer.	Employer is liable under a negligence standard if the plaintiff can prove (a) the employer knew or should have known about the harassment and (b) the employer failed to take prompt remedial action.

Consider the two tests for liability for hostile environment claims. The tests are essentially asking the same questions: what did the employer do to stop or correct harassing behavior and what did the employee do to report the behavior? The issue is who has the burden of proof. For a case involving supervisors, the employer has the burden (because it is an affirmative defense). If the employer cannot meet the burden, then the plaintiff wins. For a case involving co-workers, the plaintiff has the burden of proving the employer failed to take the necessary steps.

Because liability may turn on whether the alleged harasser is a supervisor, who counts as a supervisor? In Vance v. Ball State Univ., 570 U.S. 421 (2013), the Court defined "supervisor" as someone who is "empowered by the employer to take tangible employment actions against the victim." Remember tangible employment

[16] Yes, this is why you have had harassment prevention training at all of your jobs.

actions are "a significant change in employment status, such as hiring, firing, failing to promote, reassignment with significantly different responsibilities or a decision causing a significant change in benefits."

You should also know that in 2022, Congress enacted the Speak Out Act which prohibits the use of nondisclosure and nondisparagement clauses agreed to before a suit involving sexual assault. This does not mean that such clauses can't be part of a settlement agreement under federal law. This statute builds on the prior 2022 Ending Forced Arbitration of Sexual Assault and Sexual Harassment Act (EFAA). This aptly named statute amends the Federal Arbitration Act to prohibit enforcement of pre-dispute agreements to arbitrate sexual assault or sexual harassment claims.

To summarize:

Harassment claims, a hostile environment claim may exist for any protected class under the statutes. A quid pro quo claim is based on sex only and only arises if it involves a supervisor and a tangible employment action.

CHAPTER 10

Age Discrimination

Just as we did in the last Chapter for Title VII, in this Chapter, we will discuss some of the quirks and specifics for claims under the Age Discrimination in Employment Act.

A. What's Covered?

As you learned in Chapter 2, the ADEA prohibits discrimination because of age. The Court has held that discrimination because of age means adverse action against someone who is at least 40 years old in favor of someone younger. To fall within the statute, employers must have at least 20 employees.

There is a statutory exemption for law enforcement and fire fighters. State and local governments are allowed to set age limitations for hiring and allowed to discharge after age 55.

The Court has found no age discrimination when the employer acted on the basis of pension status, even when the pension status depended, in part, on age! Kentucky Retirement System v. EEOC, 554 U.S. 135 (2008).

B. What Claims?

In considering the frameworks for proving violations of the statute, all the claims are available (including retaliation and hostile environment).[1] Even though the ADEA does not have explicit language providing a disparate impact claim, the Court in Smith v. City of Jackson, 544 U.S. 228 (2005), held that there is such a claim. Remember the *Gross v. FBL* decision—no mixed motive claims under an individual disparate treatment framework. The Supreme Court just added a wrinkle in this area under the federal employee sector provision.

In Babb v. Wilkie, 589 U.S. 399 (2020), the Court held that to be entitled to all available remedies (see Chapter 13), a plaintiff must prove that age was the "but for" cause of the decision. However, a showing that age played a lesser part in the process will entitle the federally-employed plaintiff to certain, forward looking types of relief (such as an injunction) but not reinstatement, back pay, or compensatory damages.

What does this mean? It means you hope the fact pattern on your exam is one person discriminated against on the basis of age who doesn't work for the federal government!

C. What Defenses?

The ADEA has explicit statutory language that lists "reasonable factors other than age" as a defense. This defense is available to an individual disparate treatment claim (similar to the LNDR) and the Court held in Meacham v. Knolls Atomic Power Lab., 554 U.S. 84 (2008), that the RFOA is the defense to a disparate impact claim under the ADEA. The employer has the burden of proof and the RFOA

---

[1] Because of some Con Law type decisions, state and local employees aren't able to sue their employers for monetary damages for a violation of the ADEA. They may sue for equitable remedies and the federal government may sue on their behalf.

is MUCH easier to meet than business necessity. The employer does need some sort business reason so it is slightly more difficult than a LNDR (which can be any non-discriminatory reason).

The ADEA allows a BFOQ based on age.[2] Remember that for a BFOQ, the employer has the burden of persuasion. In age-based BFOQs, the employer usually asserts some kind of safety rationale. "I can't have someone at risk for a heart attack driving my long haul truck." As long as the employer is able to meet the *Criswell* test, discussed in Chapter 3, the employer will be able to use an age-based BFOQ. Just as with BFOQs under Title VII, cost justification isn't a defense.

Two other affirmative defenses in section 4(f) are seniority systems and employee benefit plans. Let's focus on employee benefit plans. The tricky part for benefit plans is for some benefits, it costs more to provide older workers with the same level of benefits as younger workers. The ADEA deals with this by allowing employers to either spend the same amount on all employees even if it results in less benefits for older workers or provide equal benefits.

Finally, although not technically a defense (instead a way to get the case kicked out of court), courts have recognized the ministerial exception to ADEA claims.

D. Retirement

One of the most important prohibitions in the ADEA is the prohibition on mandatory retirement based on age. No mandatory retirement based on age except . . . (you knew that was coming, didn't you?) for highly paid executives, and high level policy officials. Also, remember that the ADEA allows for a BFOQ based on age.

---

[2] Section 4(f).

Voluntary retirement, on the other hand, is a whole different ball of wax. Providing early retirement incentives is not a violation of the Act because it is not discrimination in favor of someone younger. Early retirement incentive plans are lawful as long as the plan meets certain requirements in the Older Workers Benefit Protection Act (OWBPA). If accepting the incentive comes with a waiver of ADEA claims, there is an even LONGER list of requirements in OWBPA.

E. Procedural and Remedial Differences

Procedures and remedies are more fully explained in Chapters 12 and 13 but here are a few key differences:

- An ADEA complainant may pursue state and federal remedies concurrently.
- An ADEA complainant may file suit within 60 days after filing a charge without waiting for agency to issue right to sue notice.[3]
- Successful ADEA plaintiffs receive liquidated damages instead of compensatory damages and only if there is a willful violation.
- Attorney's fees are available to prevailing plaintiffs only (not defendants).

[3] Under Title VII and the ADA, an individual must wait 180 days and then request a Right to Sue letter.

CHAPTER 11

The Americans with Disabilities Act[1] (and a Little Bit About the Rehabilitation Act)

Originally enacted in 1990, Congress amended the Act in 2009. The Americans with Disabilities Act Amendment Act (ADAAA) overturned many Supreme Court cases in order to broaden coverage.

People, I'm going to be blunt. This Chapter is not so short. The ADA gets its own Chapter because the protected class analysis is very complex and because of the interaction of disabilities and work. Sometimes, disabilities are relevant to work performance. The ADA requires employers to treat individuals differently (by providing reasonable accommodations) if their disability effects their ability to work. *But* when the disability does not affect their ability to work, employers need to treat individuals with disabilities equally. Relationship status: it's complicated.

1 42 U.S.C. § 12101 et seq.

A. Defendants

This is covered in Chapter 2 but let's briefly review. The Rehabilitation Act of 1973 covers federal agencies and anyone who accepts federal funds (contractors and grantees) and prohibits these entities from acting "solely" by reason of disability. The ADA covers state and local governments, employers with 15 or more employees, unions, and employment agencies. Because the Rehabilitation Act incorporates the liability standards of the ADA, we will focus on the ADA.[2]

B. Protected Class

Buckle up. The ADA prohibits discrimination against "a qualified individual with a disability" from discrimination on the basis of said disability. A "qualified individual" means an individual with a disability who can perform the "essential functions of the job with or without reasonable accommodation." Let's break this down into two parts: individual with a disability and qualified.

The ADA excludes certain things from the definition of disability.[3] To be an individual with a present disability, an individual must have a physical or mental impairment that substantially limits a major life activity. A plaintiff might also have a record of such an impairment or be regarded as having such an impairment.

---

[2] 29 U.S.C. § 794(d).

[3] The following are excluded from the definition of disability: "transvestism, transsexualism, pedophilia, exhibitionism, voyeurism, gender identity disorders not resulting from physical impairments, or other sexual behavior disorders; compulsive gambling, kleptomania, or pyromania; or psychoactive substance use disorders resulting from current illegal use of drugs." 42 U.S.C. § 12211(b).

1. Actual Present Disability

In Bragdon v. Abbott, 524 U.S. 624 (1998), the Court made clear that each element of the definition of the protected class must be considered.[4]

a) Physical & Mental Impairment

Under the regulations adopted by the EEOC, a physical or mental impairment includes "any physiological disorder or condition, cosmetic disfigurement, or anatomical loss affecting one or more body systems" and "any mental or psychological disorder." However, certain conditions are excluded from being an impairment.[5] A few things to keep in mind:

> Temporary impairments: A temporary impairment might be an actual, present disability (assuming the other parts of the test are met). For example, heart surgery is a serious impairment even though it lasts less than six months. However, "transitory and minor impairments" are not covered under the other two prongs or the protected class.
>
> Pregnancy: A typical pregnancy is not considered an impairment. However, a pregnancy-related impairment (like gestational diabetes) might be a disability under the "actual, present" prong if it meets the other elements of the test.

---

[4] In this case, the Court determined that an asymptomatic HIV+ person is an individual with a disability as HIV is an impairment from the moment of infection which substantially limits the major life activity of sexual activity and reproduction.

[5] Height, weight, and eye color that are in the normal range are not impairments under the statute. Common personality traits, illiteracy, and economics disadvantages are also not impairments. 29 C.F.R. pt. 1630. Further, homosexuality and bisexuality are not impairments (and therefore not disabilities) under the language of the ADA. 42 U.S.C. § 12211(a).

"Voluntary" impairments: Employers have argued that impairments which are the result of voluntary action (lung cancer as a result of smoking) should be excluded. Courts have rejected this argument (it's a slippery slope, my friends).

Contagious conditions: When considering a condition that is contagious (like tuberculosis or HIV), the Supreme Court has stated that the contagion and the physical impairment result from the same underlying condition. In other words, taking action against someone because of the contagious nature of their disease is the same as taking action against them on the basis of disability.

Once you have identified the physical or mental impairment you need to consider substantially limited.

b) Substantially Limited

Currently, the test for "substantially limits" comes from the EEOC regulations (there's no definition in the ADA itself—shocking!). To understand the current test, it's important to understand the *old* test. In Toyota Motor Manufacturing v. Williams, 534 U.S. 184 (2002), the Court defined the statutory term "substantially limits" to mean "prevents or severely restricts" on a permanent or long-term basis. As part of the move to broaden coverage, Congress overturned this decision in the 2009 Amendments and instructed the EEOC to develop new regulations (without defining the term in the statute).

Under the regulation, "substantially limited" is an individualized assessment of whether the impairment limits the ability of an individual to perform a major life activity *as compared to most people in the general population.* More specifically, the impairment does not need to prevent or severely restrict the major life activity at issue.[6]

You should consider whether an individual has a substantially limiting impairment *without* regard to mitigating measures. Medication, a prosthetic, hearing devices, assistive devices are prime examples of mitigating measures. Overruling yet another Supreme Court case, the ADA now requires courts to consider substantially limited without regard to any mitigating measures. In other words, consider the employee without his medication for hypertension. Would he be substantially limited due to his high blood pressure?

UNLESS the mitigating measures are glasses or contacts. In that case, Congress decreed, consider the glasses or contacts. (Look around at your classmates and you will understand why Congress made this exception). Keep in mind that considering mitigating measures means that fewer people will be considered substantially limited. So, *not* considering mitigating measures meets Congress' goal of broadening coverage under the Act.

One quirk for substantially limiting deals with the major life activity of working. To be substantially limited in the major life activity of working, you must be unable to work in a broad class of jobs. It has to be a big class of jobs—for example, pilot as opposed to commercial airline pilot. In Sutton v. United Air Lines, Inc., 527 U.S. 471 (1999), the Court set forth factors to consider:

- Geographical area
- Number of jobs available
- Type of jobs available

---

[6] The EEOC regulations make clear that, for some impairments, it should be easily concluded that certain impairments will at minimum substantially limit major life activities. Two quick examples: Deafness will substantially limit the major life activity of hearing; and Blindness will substantially limit the major life activity of seeing. 29 C.F.R. 1630.2(j)(3)(iii).

Finally, an impairment that is in remission (or episodic) will be considered a disability if it would be substantially limiting impairment when active.

c) Major Life Activity

To be within the protected class, an individual needs to substantially limited in at least one major life activities. (She could, of course, be limited in more than one.) The original version of the ADA didn't define the term major life activities (what??). Now the statute includes a list of activities that meet the test:

> caring for oneself, performing manual tasks, seeing, hearing, eating, sleeping, walking, standing, lifting, bending, speaking, breathing, learning, reading, concentrating, thinking, communicating, and working.[7]

Further, the ADA now lists "major bodily functions" as a major life activity.[8] This means that impairments such as diabetes may substantially limit the major life activity of the functioning of the endocrine system and therefore be considered a disability.

In the activity of performing manual tasks, the Court has held that the manual tasks have to be "central to daily life," not simply specialized tasks for the job at issue. In other words, many smaller tasks cannot be aggregated together to equal a major life activity.

To summarize:

Physical or mental impairment that

Substantially Limits

One or more Major Life Activities

---

[7] 42 U.S.C. § 12102(2)(A).

[8] 42 U.S.C. § 12102(2)(B). This includes "functions of the immune system, normal cell growth, digestive, bowel, bladder, neurological, brain, respiratory, circulatory, endocrine, and reproductive functions."

But wait! There's more.

2. Record of Such Impairment

An individual might fall within the protected class because he has a record of "such an impairment," meaning, a physical or mental impairment that substantially limits a major life activity. So what kinds of records are we talking about?:

- Employment Records
- Medial Records
- Hospitalization Stay
- Education Records

For example, a former cancer patient has a past medical history would an individual without a present disability but has a record of such an impairment. If the employer refused to hire to him because of his past history, he would fall within the protected class. Further, he could be entitled to reasonable accommodations such as time off for periodic checkups.

3. Regarded as Having Such an Impairment

The third way into the protected class is to be "regarded as having an impairment." It should come as no surprise to learn that Congress in the Amendments broadened the coverage in this category. This category is now the broadest coverage. If an individual does not need a reasonable accommodation, he should proceed under this category (because he doesn't have to prove the substantially limited element).

The ADA defines "regarded as" to include individuals who can establish that they have

> been subjected to an action prohibited under this chapter because of an actual or perceived physical or mental

impairment whether or not the impairment limits or is perceived to limit a major life activity.

Under this prong, you might have an actual impairment which doesn't substantially limit a major life activity and the employer is acting against you on the basis of your impairment or you could be not substantially limited but the employer thinks you are. You could have NO IMPAIRMENT, but the employer thinks you do and acts accordingly.

Wait, what? What does this mean? Imagine Rudolph the Red-Nosed Reindeer.[9] He does not have actual impairment but Santa believes he does and won't hire him. Even if having a red nose is an impairment, he is not substantially limited but Santa won't hire him because of the impairment.[10] If the ADA applied to reindeer,[11] Rudolph would fall within the protected class.

The "regarded as" prong is very broad and is intended to protect people who lose job opportunities because of employers' beliefs in this area. There are two restrictions to keep in mind.

- If you fall into the protected class because you are "regarded as" having such an impairment you are *not* entitled to reasonable accommodations.
- Under the "regarded as" prong, transitory and minor impairments lasting less than six months are *not* covered.

To summarize some more:

The protected class covers someone who

- Presently has a physical or mental impairment that substantially limits a major life activity, OR

---

[9] Imagine watching TV with me. My children deserve your empathy.

[10] Until there's a storm, of course.

[11] It does not.

- Has a record of such an impairment, OR
- Is regarded as having such an impairment.

4. Qualified Individual

All of the above—that's the FIRST part of the definition of the protected class for the ADA. To fully fall within the protected class, an individual must be *qualified*. The ADA defines "qualified" as "an individual who, with or without reasonable accommodations, can perform the essential functions" of the job. If a function is not "essential," and the individual cannot perform it, then he remains qualified. Only the *essential* functions must be meet.

In Stanley v. City of Sanford, 145 S. Ct. 2058 (2025), the Court interpreted the requirement of "qualified individual" to rule out a claim by a retiree. There, the plaintiff was a firefighter who retired due to Parkinson's disease and, under the City's policy at the time, received 75% of her health insurance policy payments. After her retirement, the City changed its health insurance policy for retirees to the detriment of those who retired due to medical reasons. The Court held that, to bring a claim under the Americans with Disabilities Act, a plaintiff must hold or desire to hold a position for which they are able to perform the essential functions of the job. Because the plaintiff wasn't able to perform the job, wasn't seeking the job, and didn't currently hold the job, she was not within the protected class.

I have found that students sometimes are very confused about the "with or without reasonable accommodation" phrase. So before we proceed any further, let's clear that up. An individual might be considered someone with a disability and is able to perform the job at issue without any changes or modifications. This person would be qualified *without* any accommodations. Another individual, say a financial analyst, might have a vision impairment. However, there is a software program that will read the documents aloud. The software program would be a reasonable accommodation and *with* this reasonable accommodation, the individual will be qualified.

The ADA states the employer's judgment as to what functions are essential shall be given "consideration" and further, a written job description is considered evidence of the essential functions.[12] Further, an individual is qualified if he can satisfy the requisite skill, experience, education, and other job-related requirements. If the job is financial analyst, the individual must have the training and skills for that position. To determine whether a function is essential, courts consider the actual functioning of the job. Is the function actually something an employee must be able to perform? This does not mean that the function is performed on a daily basis. For example, an employer might require that lifeguards are able to administer CPR. Someone might go for months on the job and never administer CPR. However, it is still an essential function of the job (one would hope).

One interesting essential function is attendance in the workplace. If being in the physical workplace is an essential function, then employers do not have to provide the accommodation of working from home. Expect this to be a hotly contested area of litigation! After all that has happened in the COVID-19 pandemic, employers will need to prove that regular and timely attendance at work is an essential function.

Once the essential functions have been determined, the concept of reasonable accommodation comes into play.

C. Reasonable Accommodation

Reasonable accommodation comes into play in a few different ways. First, to prove membership in the protected class, an individual will need to prove that she is qualified. She might be

[12] 42 U.S.C. § 12111(8).

qualified only after the employer provides a reasonable accommodation. Second, a failure to provide a reasonable accommodation is a separate violation of the ADA. We'll discuss that claim below.

So what counts as a Reasonable Accommodation? First of all, keep in mind that costs may be considered in deciding whether an accommodation is reasonable. Next, you could probably make a list right now and cover many of the accommodations considered reasonable. It certainly includes making the building accessible to individuals with disabilities by providing things like elevators, ramps, etc. Reasonable accommodations also include job restructuring, part-time or modified work schedules, and reassignment to a vacant position.[13] Further, the provision for aides, readers, and interpreters are also reasonable accommodations.

Despite the fact that the ADA mentions reassignment as a reasonable accommodation, in some circumstances, reassignments might conflict with assignments made under a seniority system. The Court has held that an accommodation that requires a violation of a legitimate seniority system is not a reasonable accommodation.

D. Claims

All of the claims discussed in Chapters 3, 4, and 5 are available under the ADA as well as a hostile environment claim (Chapter 9) and retaliation (Chapter 7).

Specifically on the topic of a systemic claim (either treatment or impact), the ADA prohibits using standards or criteria that have the effect of discrimination on the basis of disability[14] and "using qualification standards, employment tests or other selection

[13] VACANT. A vacant position. An employer does not need to kick an employee out of a position to make room for an individual with a disability.

[14] 42 U.S.C. § 12112(b)(3)(A).

criteria that screen out or tend to screen out an individual with a disability."[15]

Retaliation is prohibited by the ADA by the statutory language. The provision is a little different from Title VII and the ADEA because it also applies to coercing, intimidating, threatening, or interfering with the ADA on behalf of the individual or another.

The ADA allows for hostile environment claims. A plaintiff could bring a hostile environment claim because he is being harassed because he has a disability.

The ADA protects certain relationships. These are known as associational discrimination claims. In fancy terms, an employer cannot discriminate against someone "because of the known disability of an individual with whom the qualified person has a relationship or association."[16] Let's say Jane is a qualified employee. Her son has a disability and the employer is aware of this disability. If the employer fires Jane because he has concerns about her son's disability (maybe the employer doesn't want to pay for health care for the son or thinks Jane won't be devoted to her job), then Jane has a claim for associational discrimination. Reasonable accommodations are *not* available for this type of claim. The only possible defense is direct threat (discussed below).

Failure to provide a reasonable accommodation is a separate claim under the ADA. The employer has an obligation to accommodate the known physical and mental limitations of a qualified employee unless there is an undue hardship. The employee must show that an accommodation is reasonable and then the employer has the burden to prove that the accommodation proposed is an undue hardship (see below). U.S. Airways, Inc. v. Barnett, 535 U.S. 391 (2002). The ADA envisions an interactive process for

---

[15] 42 U.S.C. § 12112(b)(6).

[16] 42 U.S.C. § 12112(b)(4).

reasonable accommodations. An employee should let the employer know of her limitations and request an accommodation. Absent a formal request, if the employer is aware of a need, it will need to provide a reasonable accommodation.

To summarize:

All the main claims PLUS:

- failure to provide a reasonable accommodation
- associational discrimination

E. Defenses

Some of the defense available under the ADA are the same as with Title VII. Just as with Title VII, if the plaintiff alleges an individual disparate treatment claim, then the employer may produce a legitimate non-discriminatory reason. In response to the screening standards and criteria mentioned above, the employer defends with business necessity and job relatedness. However, there are a few defenses unique to the ADA.[17]

1. Undue Hardship

An employer is not obligated to provide a reasonable accommodation if it would amount to an undue hardship. For example, an applicant might say "I am qualified as long as you provide me with a sign language interpreter." The employer might say "that would be an undue hardship for my workplace." The statutory definition of undue hardship is an accommodation requiring *significant difficulty or expense.*

This is a much more difficult standard to meet than undue hardship for religious accommodation (Chapter 9). Although the

[17] Additional defenses to such criteria include if the criteria is required by a federal statute or is necessary to prevent a direct threat to the health and safety of others.

employee may point to the cost of the accommodation, the ADA requires significant expense (rather than de minimis for a religious accommodation). The burden is on the employer to show that the proposed accommodation is an undue hardship. The ADA provides a number of factors to consider, chiefly among them the size and financial resources of the employer. This means the same accommodation might be an undue hardship for an employer with 17 employees but not for a 500+ employee company.

2. Direct Threat

Another statutory defense is "direct threat." A direct threat can disqualify an individual from proving he is qualified. The ADA defines direct threat as a significant risk to the health and safety of other individuals in the workplace. The employer can't just wake up and decide that someone is a direct threat. The assessment must be made on the basis of objective medical judgement. The ADA provides factors to consider in deciding if an impairment is a direct threat:

- Duration of the Risk
- Nature and Potential Harm
- Likelihood of Potential Harm
- Imminence of the Potential Harm

You are also considering the job at issue as well. For example, an impairment in a surgical technician might be a direct threat but not for a school teacher.

Despite the wording of the defense—"direct threat to the health and safety of others"—the Court upheld an EEOC interpretation that expanded the defense to the health of the employee herself. Chevron, U.S.A. Inc. v. Echazabal, 536 U.S. 73 (2002).

To summarize defenses:

LNDR

Business necessity and job relatedness

Undue Hardship

Direct threat (to self or others in the workplace)

F. Special Problems Under Disability Discrimination

1. Drug and Alcohol Users

The ADA does protect alcoholics and drug addicts from discrimination on the basis of their alcoholism or addiction. That doesn't mean an employer can't prohibit drinking at work. An employer may fire an employee for being under the influence of alcohol at work.

Current users of illegal drugs are excluded from coverage. If the drug use is sufficiently recent to justify the employer's belief that drug use remained an on-going problem, then the drug use is "current."

However, the protection for addiction or alcoholism means that the employer may have to make reasonable accommodations. For example, an accommodation might be to allow the employee to attend meetings during the work day.

2. Medical Exams and Inquiries

Many of you have had a medical inquiry and didn't even realize it. If you have applied for a job in retail or the service industry and been asked if you are able to stand for 8 hours, that is a medical inquiry about your physical ability to do that job. If the inquiry occurs prior to starting the job, an employer may inquire into the ability of an applicant to perform the job. For example, are you able to carry the Employment Discrimination casebook AND the statutory supplement AND your notes AND your laptop? The employer may condition an offer of employment on the results of a medical exam on two conditions: all new employees have to take the exam and the results are kept confidential.

Note: Testing for illegal drug use is NOT considered a medical exam.

The law is a little different for current employees. Employers are prohibited from requiring medical exams or inquiries of employees unless it is job related and business necessity. If the employer has a reasonable objective concern about the employee's ability to do the job, the employer is able to require a medical exam but, as with applicants, the results must be confidential.

One last thing to keep in mind:

If the Family and Medical Leave Act applies,[18] the employer must provide up to twelve weeks of leave when the employee is unable to work due to a serious health condition. Because of this, the FMLA may cover health situations that aren't covered by the ADA.

G. Procedures and Remedies

Great news! The ADA incorporates by reference the procedures and remedies of Title VII. Nothing new to learn here. Read on to Chapters 12 and 13 for the information on procedures and remedies.

---

[18] The employer must have 50 employees.

CHAPTER 12

Procedures

Bringing one of these claims to court is a complicated process involving a state agency (most of the time), a federal agency, and finally, the court![1] To make matters more confusing, the time limits for filing are SHORT! Title VII is the standard (the ADA explicitly looks to Title VII for the procedures). The ADEA has some important differences[2] and federal employees have a different process. Although this may seem a bit mind-numbing, these administrative procedures have prevented more plaintiffs from recovering on their claims than the substantive law. So we better figure this out.

A. The Steps

Here are the basics steps:

1) File a charge with a state agency (if the state has one);

2) File charge with EEOC within the time period (more on this below);

[1] 42 U.S.C. §§ 1981 and 1983 and the Equal Pay Act do not have these administrative requirements.

[2] The remedial provisions of the Fair Labor Standards Act apply to ADEA action.

3) EEOC serves notice on the employer;

4) EEOC investigates and reaches a determination;

5) Charging party requests a Right to Sue letter (or waits for the EEOC to decide what to do);

6) File complaint in state or federal court.

Easy-peasy, right? Read on, my friends, read on.

Step 1: File with State Agency

If the state has an agency to accept complaints, this is known as a deferral state. The prospective plaintiff must file with the state agency first.[3] Each state sets its own time limits for the filing. A typical time period is six months. The EEOC has to wait for 60 days while the state agency considers the charge. This can lead to some tricky timing issues. The state agencies and the EEOC solve this with "cross-filing" and work sharing agreements. If there is a work sharing agreement and a person files with the state agency, the state agency will send a copy over to the EEOC. If a party files the EEOC first and forgets to file with the state agency, the EEOC will send the action to the state agency. The ADEA explicitly allows for a party to file with the state agency and the EEOC at the same time.

Step 2: File Charge with EEOC Within Time Period

The employee must file a charge with the EEOC within 300 days of alleged unlawful action or 30 days after state agency makes a determination or relinquishes jurisdiction WHICHEVER IS EARLIER.[4] This leads to the question of what counts as a "charge." Basically, it needs to be a statement in writing, under oath, naming the alleged violator, and the discriminatory act (a general allegation is

---

[3] Only a small number of states are non-deferral states.

[4] If there isn't a state agency, then the employee has 180 days to file with the EEOC.

enough). The Court has held that as long as the charge may be "reasonably construed as a request for the agency to take remedial action to protect the EE's rights," it will count as a charge. Federal Express v. Holowecki, 552 U.S. 389 (2008).

Step 3: EEOC Serves Notices on Employer

The EEOC serves notice on the employer within 10 days and the employer has 30 days to respond. Then the charging party (the employee) gets to submit a rebuttal to the employer's information.

Step 4: EEOC Investigates

If the EEOC finds there is no reasonable cause to believe a violation has occurred, it will dismiss the charge and issue a "Notice of Dismissal." If it finds reasonable cause, then the agency will attempt to mediate the dispute. If that doesn't work, the agency will decide whether to bring a suit itself. Otherwise, it will give the prospective plaintiff a "Right to Sue Letter."

Step 5: Charging Party Requests a Right to Sue Letter

After 180 days have passed from the filing of the charge, the charging party is able to request the Right to Sue letter. She may also wait for the EEOC to reach a decision. But once the 180 days has passed, she can always ask. In other words, it isn't a "this is your one shot" situation.

Step 6: File Complaint in State or Federal Court

Once the prospective plaintiff receives the Notice of Dismissal or the Right to Sue letter, she has 90 days to file the complaint in state or federal court. The complaint needs to be based on the allegations in the charge.

NOTE: ADEA does NOT require a Right to Sue letter in order to bring suit. Instead, a party just needs to wait 60 days from filing the charge to file the complaint in court.

B. Day Zero?

One of the trickiest questions in this area is when the time period starts running. In other words, what counts as Day Zero? The answer to that depends on the type of adverse action at issue.

Discrete acts: This applies to a single act type of employment action (hiring, firing, denial of a promotion). For discrete acts, Day Zero is the day the plaintiff has notice of the decision. Shockingly, this is known as the Notice of Decision rule. Delaware State College v. Ricks, 449 U.S. 250 (1980). It means the time period starts to run when the plaintiff knows of the adverse action, not necessarily the discriminatory intent behind the act and not when the consequences of the act became most painful. In other words, if the employer says I'm firing you and your last day is in two weeks, today is the date of the action, not in two weeks on your last day. Further, it doesn't matter that maybe you could change the employer's mind between the notice and the last day (maybe because of a grievance process), the clock still starts to run.

Hostile environment claims: As you learned in Chapter 9, hostile environment claims typically arise from multiple actions (pervasive actions). Once there are enough single acts to equate a hostile environment, is that Day Zero? The Court in National RR Passenger Corp v. Morgan, 536 U.S. 101 (2002), held that each time there is an act contributing to the hostile environment, the claim accrues. In other words, if there is an actionable claim arise after 4 incidents, a plaintiff could bring a claim. But if she doesn't and another 5 incidents occur, she has 300 days from the last incident.

Pay discrimination: In 2007, the Court ruled 5-4 that plaintiffs have 300 days from the pay-setting decision to bring a charge. Ledbetter v. Goodyear Tire & Rubber Co., 550 U.S. 618 (2007). In other words, if the plaintiff's compensation is lower because a negative performance evaluation due to discrimination, then the plaintiff has 300 days from the negative performance evaluation. This was true even if she doesn't know that the performance evaluation was lower because of discrimination. Justice Ginsburg suggested in the dissent that Congress needed to step in and fix the statute. Congress did just so in the Ledbetter Fair Pay Act. Now, each time wages, benefits or other compensation is paid and is lower due to discrimination, the time period accrues. In other words, every paycheck which is lower because of discrimination is a new day zero. But this new rule applies only to discrimination in compensation setting, not a decision which results in lower compensation (for example, not receiving a promotion).[5]

There are some equitable doctrines that will toll the time period.

C. Federal Employees

The procedures are different for federal employees.[6] Suppose Paula is demoted by the SEC.[7] Within 45 days of being demoted, Paula has to contact the Equal Employment Officer at the SEC. Then, the SEC investigates. If the SEC investigation determines that

---

5 A few more rules: facially discriminatory practices may be challenged at any time; discriminatory seniority systems may be challenged whenever they affect individuals; a constructive discharge claims begins to run once the plaintiff resigns, Green v. Brennan, 578 U.S. 547 (2016); a disparate impact claim accrues on the date the employer gives the test (or uses the requirement) and every date the employer hires someone based on the results of the test, Lewis v. City of Chicago, 560 U.S. 205 (2010); and, finally, for a pattern or practice case, when the employer refuses to hire (or fires), the time period starts.

6 Under the ADEA, a federal employee can sue after he notifies the EEOC of the intent to sue and then waits 30 days.

7 The Securities and Exchange Commission, not the athletic league.

there isn't a violation, Paula may request a hearing before an EEOC administrative law judge. Or Paula may request a final decision by the SEC. After the SEC's final decision, Paula has 90 days to file her complaint in state or federal court. Just as with non-federal employees, Paula may decide to file suit after 180 days have passed.

CHAPTER 13

Remedies

What happens if a plaintiff wins? What remedies are available? Keep in mind as you read about the particular remedies that it's the employer that is on the hook, not individual supervisors.[1]

The big idea here is to make a successful plaintiff whole, to put him in the position he would have been in but for the discrimination. This is sometimes called "make whole relief." The award of remedies is discretionary in the trial judge but the Court has set out some strong suggestions. The remedies can be grouped into two broad categories: equitable relief and legal relief.

A. Equitable Relief

The statutes all provide for various types of equitable relief, such as reinstatement and hiring. When courts award this type of relief, they consider the current employees and try to avoid displacing or bumping current workers.

Seniority is a type of equitable remedy. Sometimes this is referred to as "retroactive seniority" or "rightful place" seniority.

1 Some state laws do have personal liability by supervisors or employees. This is not the case under the federal statutes.

Basically, this means that the successful plaintiff's place in the seniority line-up should be considered as the date they lost seniority because of the discrimination. Even though this does impact other workers who will move down the bidding list (for example), the Court in Franks v. Bowman Transportation, 424 U.S. 747 (1976), held that make whole relief requires this type of remedial seniority.

Backpay is the equitable remedy that really packs a punch. Because the Court considers this an equitable type of relief, the determination of back pay is decided by the Court and isn't subject to the cap discussed below. It's available under Title VII, ADA, FMLA, and the Equal Pay Act.

In Albemarle Paper Co. v. Moody, 422 U.S. 405 (1975), the Court held that although backpay is not mandatory or automatic, when considering the purposes of the Act, there is a presumption of back pay. Backpay doesn't just mean wages. Backpay includes all the compensation a successful plaintiff would have received in the absence of discrimination (wages, raises, overtime, benefits, vacation pay, retirement benefits, etc. etc. etc.!). Plus, the backpay award comes with prejudgment interest from the date of the unlawful employment action. This can be a HUGE amount of money.

There are some limits on backpay. Backpay starts on the date the plaintiff first lost wages but can't go back more than two years prior to the filing of a charge. The time period stops typically on the date of judgment but it might be stopped by other events.[2] Further, the backpay amount will be reduced by any wages that the plaintiff did earn and an amount that the plaintiff could have earned with

[2] The backpay period can stop if the plaintiff resigns or turns down offer of reinstatement or dies or would have been laid off. It can also be cut off by something known as "after acquired evidence." Suppose the employer fired the plaintiff because of his religion. Then, AFTER that decision, the employer finds evidence that the plaintiff was stealing from the employer. Because the employer didn't know this at the time of the decision to fire the plaintiff, it is still liable but the remedies are limited.

"reasonable diligence." In other words, the plaintiff has to go get a job and try and make some money.

Front pay is another remedy available. It's a little wacky. Imagine that the court says you are entitled to reinstatement but there is no vacancy; front pay carries you over until you get the position. But if reinstatement is never possible (because the employer and the plaintiff hate each other), then front pay is damages in lieu of reinstatement. Because make whole relief is the guiding principle, the front pay calculation can be pretty complex. A front pay can include total future salary, pension benefits (etc. etc. etc.) from date of judgment until the probable loss of job or retirement! Just as with backpay, there is a duty to mitigate. A front pay award will be reduced by the amount the plaintiff will earn in whatever job she has secured.

B. Legal Relief

In the now famous 1991 Amendments, Congress added the ability to obtain compensatory and punitive damages under Title VII and ADA claims (but not under the ADEA or the Equal Pay Act). These damages are available for intentional discrimination claims only (i.e. treatment claims and only as long as the employer hasn't proven the "same decision" defense) and Congress added a cap on damages based on the number of employees.[3]

$50,000 for employers with 15-100 employees

$100,000 for employers with 101-200 employees

$200,000 for employers with 201-500 employees

$300,000 for employers with 501 or more employees

---

[3] Because backpay and front pay aren't considered compensatory damages, these amounts don't fall under the cap.

1. *Compensatory Damages*

What counts as compensatory damages? Many, many things: mental distress; lost earning capacity; inconvenience; medical expenses; the costs of looking for new employment, (etc. etc. etc.).

2. *Punitive Damages*

Punitive damages are available when some agent of the employer acted with "malice or reckless indifference to the federally protected rights" of the plaintiff and the employer is liable for that person's actions. Kolstad v. American Dental Association, 527 U.S. 526 (1999). This means that there is a good faith defense is available to a punitive damages claim.

3. *Liquidated Damages*

Liquidated damages means the statute has set the amount. Liquidated damages are the amount of the unpaid (or lost) wages. A successful plaintiff gets double backpay. The Equal Pay Act and the FMLA automatically award liquidated damages and the ADEA allows an award if the violation of the statute was "willful." If a willful violation is proven, the liquidated damages MUST be awarded. A violation is willful if the employer knew or was reckless that its action violated the statute.

4. *Attorney's Fees*

The very last thing under remedies is attorneys' fees. The big question here is whether it is "attorneys' fees" or "attorney's fees." Not really.

In most litigation in the U.S. system, everyone pays their own way. The anti-discrimination statutes are an exception. Fees may be awarded to a "prevailing party." They are almost always awarded to a prevailing plaintiff.[4] This means the plaintiff won some judgment from the court (even if just nominal damages). A successful defendant might be awarded fees but it will need to show that the plaintiff's action was frivolous, unreasonable, or without foundation.

---

4 In fact, the ADEA allows a fee award to plaintiffs only.

CHAPTER 14

What's New? All the Acronyms

In addition to the Supreme Court decisions, legislation, and Executive Orders already mentioned, a few other areas are hot topics in the world of Employment Discrimination: DEI, COVID, and AI.

A. DEI

Much has happened in the area of Diversity, Equity, and Inclusion over the past five years.[1] What is DEI? A proponent of DEI initiatives would define it as promoting inclusive workplaces by removing systemic barriers to advancement and creating policies to help all employees to thrive. Whereas a critic of such programs might challenge DEI initiatives as unlawfully considering race or sex in workplace decisions, resulting in unqualified people gaining jobs or promotions.

In recent years, a wide variety of employers (including law firms) have faced challenges over diversity hiring programs. Winston Strawn, Morrison & Foerster, and Perkins Coie were all challenged

[1] Sometimes known as DEIA: Diversity, Equity, Inclusion, and Accessibility.

for their fellowship program designed to foster diversity after the firm altered its application criteria. The claims alleged that these fellowships for "disadvantaged and/or historically underrepresented group in the legal profession" violate 42 U.S.C. § 1981, because the law firms are expressly refusing to contract with certain applicants based on their race and ethnicity. The lawsuits were dropped or never brought when firms changed the criteria for the programs.[2]

In what is now a familiar story, the first Trump Administration issued an executive order to revoke equity programs within the federal government. The Biden Administration revoked that order and required federal agencies to engage in an equity review for each agency's programs. The second Trump Administration played the UNO reverse card and revoked the order revoking the previous order.[3] The most recent Executive Order (entitled Ending Radical And Wasteful Government DEI Programs And Preferencing) requires the cessation of all equity programs, offices, and positions within federal agencies.

In a separate Executive Order (Ending Illegal Discrimination and Restoring Merit-Based Opportunity), the Trump Administration ordered "all executive departments and agencies (agencies) to terminate all discriminatory and illegal preferences, mandates, policies, programs, activities, guidance, regulations, enforcement actions, consent orders, and requirements." This order also revoked a prior EO requiring federal contractors to follow certain affirmative action guidelines. This Executive Order also required agencies to take action to encourage private sector to cease the use of DEI

---

[2] Other lawsuits brought by non-profit groups against private employers for hiring or promotion practices were dismissed for a lack of standing. Some remain active.

[3] There is an endless supply of UNO reverse cards.

policies and preferences, including creating a list of possible litigation targets.[4]

As is to be expected, these Orders have been challenged in litigation with a wide variety of results.[5]

B. COVID

I know, I know. We are all still have PTSD from the pandemic days. Although the pandemic raised many, many, many employment law issues,[6] in the area of employment discrimination, the primary issues focus on religious and disability discrimination claims. Although it seems long ago, there is on-going litigation over employer COVID policies.

Even in the absence of federal or state requirements for masking, many employers required employees to mask in the workplace. These masking requirements faced challenges as a burden on employees' religious beliefs. In addition, employees requested an exemption from the mask mandate as an accommodation for a disability. Vaccination requirements faced similar challenges.

As discussed in Chapter 9, employers have an obligation to reasonably accommodate employees' religious observances unless there is an undue hardship (now defined as significant difficulty or expense). Employees must show that masking or vaccination conflicts with a religious belief. In other words, to succeed on a religious exemption claim, employees must show that the belief is sincerely held and that it is religious in nature. Many plaintiffs' claims in this area failed on this prong: courts did not credit the

---

4 Veterans' preferences are exempt.

5 Several organizations, including law firms and nonprofits, are tracking the litigation brought against these executive orders. If you are interested in the latest updates, I suggest using one of these sources!

6 No, HIPAA does not prohibit the door checker at the grocery store from asking you to wear a mask.

assertions that their religious beliefs formed the basis for the opposition to masks or vaccinations.

If the employee does meet these requirements, an employer may be able to show that allowing an employee to remain unmasked is an undue burden.[7] Employers often assert a safety issue for unmasked or unvaccinated employees. However, employers must also consider whether there is a reasonable accommodation. For example, an employer might grant the exemption from vaccination but then require the employee to submit to weekly testing. Employees often suggest working from home as a reasonable accommodation. Whether working from home is a viable accommodation will depend entirely on the job at issue!

As for disability accommodations, the employee must prove that they are an individual with a disability that is qualified to perform the essential functions of the job and the disability prevents them from wearing a mask or being vaccinated. This requires documentation from a healthcare provider of the employee's medical condition that counsels against vaccination, such as an allergy to the components of the vaccine or a prior adverse reaction to a vaccine. Even if the medical condition is documented, the employer may refuse the accommodation if doing so would create an undue hardship.

Before COVID, employees with disabilities requested the ability to work from home as an accommodation. Courts typically found that employers did not have to offer such an accommodation because it would be undue burden. How could someone be supervised when they are working from home?? Will they just be in

[7] On the flip side of the COVID mask requirements is a new set of laws forbidding masking. However, these bans apply primarily to public spaces. If an employer adopted a policy of a mask ban, they would need to offer the same exemptions for religious and disability accommodations.

their jammies streaming Love Island all day?[8] Well, you can imagine that after so many people worked from home for months (or years), disability rights advocates are now pointing out the feasibility of such arrangements. The EEOC published guidance stating that employers could "reassess" the accommodations offered to determine if such accommodations were still necessary but could not simply terminate all accommodations. Some courts have held that workplace accommodations created in a national emergency do not bind employers when the emergency is over. Employers, of course, are free to grant these accommodations if they wish. AOTW, the trend is now "return to work."

Finally, another issue from the COVID times is the existence of Long COVID. The EEOC issued guidance acknowledging Long COVID as a disability and suggesting the types of accommodations that might be necessary. These, of course, are dependent on the manifestations of COVID in the individual employee. For example, someone who suffers from brain fog might request a quiet work space. Or someone with headaches might request different lighting.

C. AI

Ugh, screening resumes takes *forever!* Many employers have turned to artificial intelligence to play a larger and larger role in the hiring process. These tools, however, may be another source of discriminatory actions. One infamous resume screening tool created an algorithm for the two factors most indicative of success on the job: the name Jared and playing lacrosse in high school.[9] This has launched many articles discussing the discrimination that might occur from using AI and how to avoid it.

---

[8] Or making themselves French toast for breakfast during their ACTUAL French class as my children (then in high school) did.

[9] Dave Gershgorn, *Companies are on the hook if their hiring algorithms are biased,* https://qz.com/1427621/companies-are-on-the-hook-if-their-hiring-algorithms-are-biased (update June 22, 20, 2022)

In 2023, the EEOC issued guidance on the use of AI or other similar technology when used by employers to make or inform employment decisions such as hiring or promotions. The technology at issue includes resume screeners looking for certain words, video interviews, and chatbots. The guidance focused on the possibility of disparate impact against a protected class with specific discussion of individuals with disabilities.[10] This guidance is no longer available on the EEOC website. However, it is possible for private plaintiffs to bring a claim of discrimination based on the use of AI tools.

---

[10] Recall that President Trump has issued an Executive Order to agencies to reject the use of disparate impact analysis.